D1571840

DEMPSEY
IN
Nevada

DEMPSEY
IN
Nevada

By Guy Clifton

Jack Bacon & Company
Reno, Nevada
2007

Baobab Books
Nevada

ISBN 0-930083-33-4

Jack Bacon & Company
516 South Virginia Street
Reno, Nevada 89501
www.JackBacon.com

For my friend Mick Laxalt

In memory of Rollan Melton, Ty Cobb and Robert Laxalt
Great Nevada writers who loved the fight game

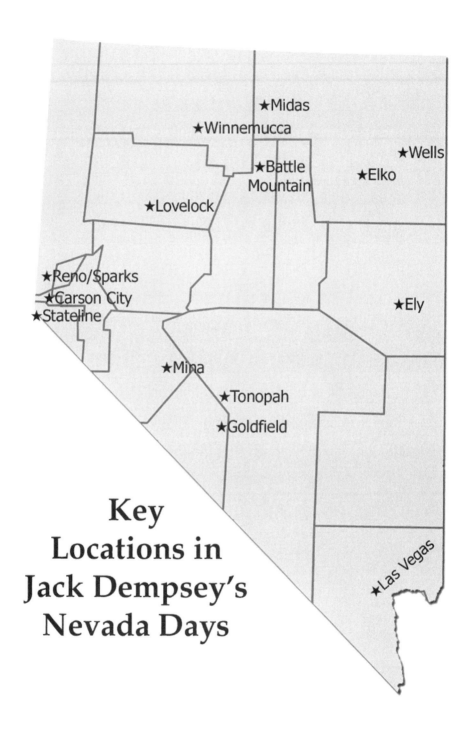

★Midas

★Winnemucca

★Wells

★Battle
Mountain

★Elko

★Lovelock

★Reno/Sparks
★Carson City
★Stateline

★Ely

★Mina

★Tonopah

★Goldfield

★Las Vegas

Key
Locations in
Jack Dempsey's
Nevada Days

Table of Contents

Foreword
By Steve Sneddon

Walk down Reno's East Fourth Street and it's easy to imagine Jack Dempsey could be coming out a doorway anytime.

The street is Reno's time capsule and Dempsey is tightly locked into it. He first walked down that street as a young man, long before he won the world heavyweight championship. One of his fights was in a make-shift stadium a half block off the street.

As he grew older, he never forgot Reno, returning again and again. And Reno never forgot him.

No fighter, not even Jack Johnson, quite measured up to Dempsey.

Johnson brought the world to Reno in 1910 for a stroll down East Fourth Street to a fight with James J. Jeffries in what is now a salvage yard. But Johnson was gone soon after the bout. Dempsey stuck around in hearts and minds.

Dempsey didn't die in Nevada. But I like to say I attended his memorial service in Reno.

The late bar owner Dick Evans, who had been the No. 8 middleweight in the world in the 1920s, was Dempsey's long-time friend. Evans told me countless stories about Dempsey over the years. Evans made you feel like you were sitting next to Dempsey when he told those stories.

When Dempsey died, I called Evans, who was getting on in years. I took Evans to a video store and we watched Dempsey fight films. I saw visions of the 1920s and '30s sparkle in his eyes. Tears streamed down Evans' cheeks. Clearly, the vivid memories came back to Evans.

He told stories, a few I remembered and more that I didn't recall. I had to dab away the tears, too.

By the time we left that store, we were both crying. I always wondered how we had impacted the store's business that day when someone walked in to see two grown men coming out bawling.

But it might have been the best wake I've ever attended.

It was therapeutic, I think, for Evans and me.

Often over the years when we talked about Dempsey, Evans told me somebody ought write a book about Dempsey. Evans suggested I should write one. I pointed out to him that there had been a lot of books written about Dempsey and there was nothing new to be written.

Well, I was wrong.

Boy, was I wrong.

A couple of years ago, when Guy Clifton told me he was writing a book about Dempsey, I still hadn't seen the error of my ways.

But page by page, I saw the light as Guy's project progressed as nugget after nugget of information was slowly built into a treasure. The words tell a story that needed to be told one more time – and, in some cases, for the first time. Limiting the focus to Dempsey in Nevada is a masterstroke.

And the photos, oh those photos, offer glimpses of Dempsey that haven't been seen publicly.

This isn't a book. Like East Fourth Street, it's a time capsule that needed to be opened to let out Dempsey.

Steve Sneddon is the boxing writer for the Reno Gazette-Journal *and has covered hundreds of championship fights in his 40-year career. He was inducted into the Nevada Newspaper Hall of Fame in 2005.*

Introduction

Jack Dempsey left footprints all over Nevada.

He lived in a dugout cave in Goldfield and a mansion on California Avenue in Reno. He picked potatoes in Dayton, lived in Wells with his first wife, divorced his second wife in Reno, married his third in Elko and accompanied his fourth to Reno so she could get divorced from her first husband. He fought an exhibition in Sparks and scrapped for food in Goldfield, Tonopah, Mina and Ely. He fought in Reno as the No. 1 contender for the heavyweight crown in 1918 and as part of a short-lived comeback attempt in 1931. He lived, trained and prospected in Midas. He promoted a fight and helped open casinos in Las Vegas. He caught trout from the Truckee River.

One thing he never did, even though the myth persists, is work as a saloon bouncer. "Maybe the story came out of the fact that I lived in, and off, saloons for pretty nearly six years," he wrote in his 1959 autobiography. "I fought in saloons. I couldn't guess how many fights I had in saloons."

When he first showed up in Reno in April of 1915, he was an unknown hobo kid with holes in his shoes. When he returned in 1931, he was an American icon, one of the most famous people in the country.

"When you talk about the 1920s, there are three great names that stand out: Babe Ruth, Dempsey and Red Grange," said Dick Davies, a professor of history at the University of Nevada, Reno and author of the book *Sports in American Life: A History*. "Those are the big three that are always mentioned."

Dempsey quickly endeared himself to Nevadans – cops, gangsters, governors, gamblers, miners, mayors, bankers, boxers, newspapermen, cowboys and kids. He spoke to service clubs, promoted the area and was even selected as a delegate to the state Republican convention in 1932. In the spring of 1932, after months on the road fighting exhibitions for a planned comeback, he told Reno reporters: "It's good to be home."

He helped prolong the life of the Tonopah & Goldfield Railroad and testified on behalf of his friend, Hank Greenspun, when the Las Vegas newspaper publisher was on trial for transporting weapons to Palestine. In 1950, Dempsey returned to Tonopah for the town's 50th birthday celebration and was feted as honorary mayor. Governors, senators and congressmen were there, but Dempsey was the star attraction.

If Dempsey loved Nevada, the feeling was mutual. During his comeback tour in 1931, Dempsey was scheduled to fight a Labor Day bout in Reno. Full-page advertisements ran in both the *Reno Evening Gazette* and *Nevada State Journal* promoting the bout that would feature "Our Jack" Dempsey.

For a time, he was *our* Jack. And he can be found in the Silver State still today – more than 90 years after his first Nevada fight and more than 20 years after his death at age 87 in 1983. The Mizpah Hotel in Tonopah has its Jack Dempsey Room. A large photo of the champ hangs in the restaurant of the Mozart Cafe in Goldfield. A small museum in Midas has photographs of the great Manassa Mauler, as does the Nevada Hotel in Ely and the Little Nugget in downtown Reno. He lives in the archives of the Nevada Historical Society, in the stories of long-time Nevadans interviewed by the University of Nevada Oral History Program, in the personal papers of past Nevada governors, in still-standing brick homes in Reno's mansion district, in possessions passed down through generations of Nevadans, in the microfilm of a dozen Nevada newspapers and in the memories of a handful of old-timers who knew him personally.

This book is not a biography of Jack Dempsey. Several of them, and two autobiographies, have been written about the man's life. We'd recommend *A Flame of Pure Fire: Jack Dempsey and the Roaring '20s* by Roger Kahn (1999); *Jack Dempsey: The Manassa Mauler* by Randy Roberts (1979); *Dempsey: By the Man Himself* by Bob Considine and Bill Slocum (1959) or *Dempsey* by Jack Dempsey and Barbara Piatelli Dempsey (1977), for a more complete look at his life.

This book focuses on Dempsey's days in Nevada. However, it also includes chapters on parts of his life that happened outside the Silver State – his victory over the giant Jess Willard to win the heavyweight championship in 1919; his victory over French war hero Georges Carpentier in "the Battle of the Century," and his fights with Gene Tunney, in which he lost the title but won the hearts of the American people. His story simply cannot be told without them. And, as you will see, there are Nevada connections to all.

Dempsey was, officially at least, a Nevadan for only a short time, but throughout his life, he represented the qualities that most Nevadans hold dear. He asked no favors, worked hard, maintained his independence and a live-and-let-live attitude. He loved the wide-open life of the cities and the solitude of the mountains and desert. Most of all, he loved the people. His final trips to Nevada were to visit old friends and made with no press or fanfare.

When he died on May 31, 1983, newspapermen reminisced and old men wept because a part of their own history died that day as well. The Jack Dempsey of their minds was the hungry young kid who could slay giants with his fists and get up whenever he was knocked down.

This book is a compilation of newspaper articles, oral histories, boxing record books and personal interviews. Much of the information has been available in one form or another for years. Some of it has never been printed and some has not appeared in print for decades.

Many Nevadans today are surprised to learn that Dempsey once lived and loved and fought here. It's my hope with this book that his legacy in Nevada will never be forgotten.

Guy Clifton
Reno, Nevada

1

Riding the Rods to Reno

In April of 1915 – a few days after Jess Willard pounded Jack Johnson to win the heavyweight boxing championship of the world in Havana, Cuba – a raw-boned teenager rolled out from under a train in Reno, Nevada looking for a fight. He had ridden the rods – the narrow steel brake beams underneath Pullman cars – from Salt Lake City, a dangerous way to travel as one slip meant certain death. Still, it was the only way a flat-broke kid could avoid the railroad guards that patrolled the boxcars looking to crack the skulls of hobos who couldn't pay their way.

As the youngster had clung to the rods on this particular trip, the train passed within a few miles of the newly named mining camp of Willard in Pershing County. The mining claims were named by U.S. Sen. Tasker Oddie of Nevada in honor of Willard, the big Kansas farmer who ended the reign of Johnson, the first black heavyweight champion, who had whipped "white hope" Jim Jeffries in Reno five years earlier in a fight promoted by Tex Rickard.

The kid ate his first Reno meal in a hobo jungle before heading into town to check out the saloons and gyms in search of a boxing match. His given name was William, though his mother called him Harry, a shortened version of his middle name, Harrison. The kid preferred to be called Jack – Jack Dempsey.

No one, with the possible exception of his mother, would have guessed that day in April of 1915 that 19-year-old Jack Dempsey would be following both Willard and Jack Johnson into history and surpass them both as one of the greatest heavyweight champions of all time.

William Harrison Dempsey was born June 24, 1895 in Manassa, Colorado, the ninth child of Hyrum and Celia Dempsey. In a story his mother told for years, just before Jack was born, a salesman traded her a battered book for a glass of milk. The book was about John L. Sullivan, the Boston Strong Boy, who was the heavyweight champion in the late 1800s. Celia Dempsey later told her son, "I finished reading it just before you were born, so big and strong. I said to everybody, 'William is going to grow up to be the world's champion fighter. Just like John L. Sullivan.'"

JACK DEMPSEY

An early Dempsey promotional photo taken in 1915.
Colleen Rosencrantz Collection

Dempsey was neither a champion nor a particularly well-known fighter when he showed up in Reno in 1915. He'd been fighting since 1911, mainly in the mining camps of Colorado and Utah, and often under the name of Kid Blackie or Young Dempsey. He had two brothers who were also fighters, Bernie and Johnny, and both of them fought under the name Jack Dempsey, taking the name from the former middleweight champion of the late 1800s, Jack Dempsey the Nonpareil. Harry Dempsey started using the name "Jack" around 1914. He was using the name when he showed up in Reno in 1915.

He didn't choose Reno by chance. The town had regular fight cards at Moana Springs and on April 15, 1915, the *Nevada State Journal* carried a story that announced the formation of the Jockey Athletic Club by Jack Thurm, a manager and fight promoter. An open-air arena was being built near the Hotel Espanol at the corner of Third and Plaza streets with a seating capacity of 900. Thurm announced a fight card of two six-round bouts and two four-round battles would be held on Friday, April 23. Two days later, the *Journal* provided details of the card, which Thurm had decided to move back to April 26. Jack Boyd of Spokane would take on Antone La Grave of San Francisco in one of the six-round main events and Tommy Driscoll of Vallejo would battle Frankie Burns of New York in the other. Then came this sentence:

> "As a special preliminary, he has engaged Jack Dempsey of Butte and Manues (sic) Campbell of Los Angeles at 158 pounds."

That was the first mention of Jack Dempsey in a Reno newspaper – the first of what would end up being thousands over the next eight decades. At the time, Dempsey was simply glad to have a fight and potential payday. He detailed the circumstances in his 1959 autobiography. "I got a meal in a jungle, headed into town and cased the saloons and the gyms, and pretty soon, I had the promise of a fight with a good but real cozy fighter named Anamas Campbell, a guy about the size and color of Jack Johnson. Still, he wouldn't close the deal until he had a chance to box six or eight rounds with me in a gym. I was always a rotten gym fighter, but this time I made sure I looked bad. He gave me a good lacing."

The fight card was set and Thurm and several of his fighters went about the business of promoting the event. On April 22, that promotion took them to nearby Sparks and Durham's Saloon, where "an unusually large crowd" turned out for an exhibition boxing card. Jack Boyd, Frankie Burns and Dempsey "were the three boys who went with Thurm to Sparks to put on the exhibition. They were greeted with cheers and well received by the sports lovers of the neighboring city."

Dempsey became well known around Reno's saloons for walking in and challenging patrons to a fight – for a price. It was a tactic employed by former heavyweight champion John L. Sullivan who would enter a saloon and declare, "I can lick anyone in this bar."

Andrew Ginocchio, a blacksmith and later the longtime owner of Reno Iron Works, recalled in his University of Nevada oral history seeing a young Jack Dempsey do just that.

"I think it was around 1916 (sic) that Jack Dempsey first come to Reno. On Saturday night we used to go around town, but Becker's Saloon on Commercial Row seemed to be the most lively place that anyone would like to go in and have a glass of beer. And this man, Dempsey, come along, and he would go to the end of the bar, and then with his hand he hit on the end of the bar, and all of the glasses on the bar raised about 3 inches! And he says, 'I would fight the best man in the house!'

"The man in charge of the bar was a fellow by the name of Harry Heidtmann. He said to him, 'Now, look, if you want a drink, I'll give you what you want, but don't come around here to start any fights now.'

"Dempsey says, 'I'll take a shot of Old Crow and a beer for chase.'"

As the Reno fight card approached, Thurm split up the principals and had them working out at different times in the back of the Depot Saloon on Commercial Row. Dempsey, Burns and Boyd trained in the afternoons, while Campbell, La Grave and Driscoll – the favored fighters – worked out in the evening in front of "a packed house" of onlookers. The *Journal* reported that "Campbell in training shows that he is willing and game." Of Dempsey, it said: "Dempsey is a big, untried slugger and has been unable to find any of his sparring partners strong enough to make him let himself out." Dempsey became notorious in his championship years for pounding a succession of sparring partners.

When fight day arrived, five bouts were scheduled with Dempsey and Campbell the second fight on the card. Written accounts of the outcome vary – in his autobiography, Dempsey claimed a first-round knockout; the *Nevada State Journal* write-up and The Ring Record Book and Boxing Encyclopedia lists a third-round knockout by Dempsey and the *Reno Evening Gazette* reported a fourth-round knockout by Dempsey. The two Reno newspapers provided different details on how the bout ended.

The *Journal* had it this way:

> Jack Demsey (sic) outfought Emanuel Campbell, his colored opponent, in the three rounds their battle lasted. In the third round, following a fall to the floor by both fighters, the colored boy did not get up in time and was counted out by Referee Roy Moore. It was a popular decision.

The *Gazette* reported it differently (and somewhat prophetically in the final sentence of the paragraph):

> Emanuel Campbell, a big colored fighter, took an awful beating from Jack Dempsey and finally quit cold after running to avoid punishment. He fell to the floor in the fourth round after turning his back and running

half-way around the ring. After taking the count of eight, he got off his knees and when Dempsey made another rush at him dropped back to the floor. Referee Moore promptly declared Dempsey the winner. Dempsey showed great cleverness and aggressiveness and has a punch with either hand that makes him a dangerous opponent.

In his autobiography, Dempsey lamented that he had done too convincing of a job in dispatching Campbell. "When Anamas came to, he shook hands with me, grinned a big white-toothed grin and said to the people around us in the ring, 'I knew this white boy was just kidding in the gym. Should never have fought him.' Everybody else around Reno figured 'they should never have fought him,' too. I went back on the rods."

Though Dempsey stayed around Reno for several weeks and was reported as late as May 14 to be working out at the Pavilion at Moana Springs, he didn't have another official fight in Reno until three years later.

A note from Jack Dempsey's sister, Florence, to her children give the details of Jack Dempsey's fight against Johnny Sudenberg in Goldfield in 1915. *Colleen Rosencrantz Collection*

2

A Wheelbarrow Ride in Goldfield

The mining boomtown of Goldfield was on the world boxing map long before Jack Dempsey showed up in late May of 1915. Nine years earlier, a gambler and saloon owner named Tex Rickard placed $30,000 in gold in the window of his saloon and announced to the Police Gazette and other publications that he'd pay it to two "name" fighters who agreed to do battle in Goldfield. Lightweights Joe Gans and Battling Nelson answered the call and on a blistering hot Fourth of July in 1906, they fought 42 rounds with Gans winning on a foul.

In January 1909, Rickard promoted the world featherweight championship fight between champion Abe Attell and challenger Freddy Weeks, which Attell won by way of a 10th round knockout. Attell, considered one of the great featherweights of all time, later gained notoriety for his involvement in the 1919 Black Sox scandal that shook baseball.

Rickard, who went on to promote the Jack Johnson-Jim Jeffries heavyweight title fight in Reno in 1910, was gone from Goldfield when Dempsey arrived there in 1915. Their history together was still to be written, a few years and a few thousand miles down the road. The man promoting fights in Goldfield was Jake Goodfriend, manager of the Hippodrome Theater. In May of 1915, he was under some pressure to bring in fighters who could provide a good show for the miners and gamblers in Goldfield. As he told the *Goldfield Daily Tribune*, "there have been too many of these 'brother in law' matches and tenth round finishes after nine rounds of running and hugging, in the past." He signed Johnny Sudenberg as one of the principles for a May 31 card, but was unsure of an opponent. Jack Gilfeather, Dempsey's manager at the time, convinced the promoter to give Dempsey a shot. Goodfriend had never seen Dempsey fight, but word had trickled down from Reno that he was a game fighter, so Goodfriend arranged a test. By Dempsey's own recollection, it didn't start well.

"Goodfriend, the promoter, put me in a gym in the back of a saloon to see how I could do against a smart old negro named Slick Merrill. The combination of hunger, some recent days on the rods and Slick's good left hand had me reeling all over the place.

"'You look lousy,'" Goodfriend said from ringside, chewing a cigar."

Then fate, circumstance or pure luck intervened.

"Slick charged me, looking to knock me out. I fell into a clinch, open-mouthed, and accidentally bit a chunk out of his forehead. Blood poured down his face like a waterfall. Goodfriend signed me for the Sudenberg fight. Maybe he figured that if I couldn't fight I could at least bite."

Dempsey was guaranteed $150 for the fight and he excitedly let his family in Utah know about his bout. They were equally thrilled. His sister, Florence, sent a post card to her son, Lloyd Stannard, featuring a photo of a skinny Dempsey on the front with the name "Jack Dempsey" and a note on the back with the details.

> Lloyd and Norma.
> Do you know who this is? He is fighting in Gold-field, Nev. His big fight comes off tonight, Friday. He will make $150.00 win or loose this time – so keep this picture honey to remember Uncle Harry's fight.
> They all call themselves "Jack." Ha ha.
> Mother

State Sen. Emory Arnold was selected as the referee for the 10-round main event between Sudenberg and Dempsey. Goodfriend vowed that "if any fighter shows an inclination to stall and not give the best that is in him, the contest will be stopped immediately and the disqualified fighter's end of the purse will be given to charity."

The *Goldfield Daily Tribune* reported both fighters were well-trained and brimming with confidence. The paper favored the experienced Sudenberg.

"Sudenberg declares he will put on the fight of his life in an endeavor to flatten the boy from Pueblo. Johnnie has not lost a fight while battling around these parts and the only thing lacking in his performance is his failure to stow his opponents away. 'I'll win or lose by knockout,' said Johnnie, 'and you can bet I don't figure to lose.'"

The next day's paper revealed a different story than what Sudenberg had planned under the headline "Dempsey Looms Large in Scrap."

> For ten rounds last night Jack Dempsey of Pueblo, who looked more like an overgrown schoolboy than a fighter, and who incidentally proved otherwise, met the lunges of his shorter opponent, Johnny Sudenberg, with a straight left which invariably connected with the latter's visage before Johnny could get inside the Colorado boy's guard for a slam of his own variety."

Dempsey used his straight left and right jab to keep Sudenberg away through the first five rounds, then switched to fighting inside, with equal success, according to the *Daily Tribune's* report. Dempsey realized he could hold Sudenberg tight in the clinches "an opened up with a succession of jolts, chops and jabs with his right to Johnny's jaw, which kept the latter's head bobbing during the rest of the fight."

Sudenberg recovered by the eighth round and was giving as good as he got. "Both boys were fighting strong and furiously at the bell, and under the circumstances, the best decision that could be given was the one Referee Arnold made when he called the bout a draw."

Dempsey didn't argue. In fact, when he recalled the incident years later for his 1959 autobiography, he said he'd been knocked silly early on and didn't recall much of the fight. "Sudenberg almost killed me. For two rounds it was a fight. For the next eight, I was a helpless, blood-soaked punching bag. It was the worst beating of my life. I don't remember going down once because I still don't remember the last three or four rounds."

Dempsey said he collapsed after the fight and was unceremoniously dumped into a wheelbarrow where a good Samaritan wheeled him across town and dumped him onto his bunk in the dirt cave where he was staying because he couldn't afford a hotel room. "Goldfield had been a boom mining town and a room cost five dollars a week. In advance, for a skinny young hobo with holes in his shoes and a newspaper for a suitcase."

When he came to the following day, Dempsey went in search of his manager, Gilfeather, to collect his share of the purse. That's when he was informed Gilfeather had gotten drunk, gambled away the money in a craps game and skipped town. "I had been damn near killed for nothing," Dempsey wrote in his autobiography. "I was broke and starving. It was the lowest point of my entire life."

What Dempsey didn't know was some in the crowd that night felt he was given a bum decision and should have been declared the winner. These same people happened to be arranging a card in nearby Tonopah several days later.

Dempsey and Sudenberg were signed for a quick rematch.

3
A Tonopah Slugfest and a Stickup

Members of the newly formed Tonopah Athletic Club were impressed enough with Jack Dempsey in his fight with Johnny Sudenberg in Goldfield that they signed him the next day for a rematch with Sudenberg at the Airdome in Tonopah. The men were also disgusted with the Goldfield fight being declared a draw. The *Tonopah Daily Bonanza* reported in its June 3, 1915 edition: "Because of the fact that a great many were dissatisfied with the decision last Monday in the Dempsey-Sudenberg contest and that Dempsey gave Sudenberg the best fight he has had in this part of the country, this card for June 11 should be the best contest ever staged here."

An odd twist in the *Daily Bonanza* story is that it referred to Dempsey as being from New York. Not only had he never been to New York, he had never fought anywhere east of Colorado at this time. The Goldfield paper had referred to him being from Pueblo, while the Reno papers from a few weeks earlier said he was from Salt Lake City. The latter was probably closest to the truth since his parents were living in Utah at the time and that is where he made home base when he wasn't traveling.

Whatever the case, the rematch with Sudenberg was set as another 10-round bout and the "grand special event" to precede the Jack Bratton-Roy Moore featherweight championship match.

Dempsey, still broke and hungry after his now former manager skipped out on him, hired on as a dishwasher in saloons, which entitled him to a free lunch. Like with Goldfield, there were people in Tonopah who would one day come back into Dempsey's life. One of them was saloon owner Nick Abelman, who would become a key player when Nevada reinstated its gambling laws in 1931. Ableman was the primary fight promoter in Tonopah for many years. Later, Dempsey and Abelman would become neighbors on California Avenue in Reno when Dempsey moved to town for a divorce. In Tonopah, Abelman was associated with George Wingfield in the Big Casino and Tonopah Club. He also owned the Cobweb Saloon and other properties.

Both Dempsey and Sudenberg trained in the Big Casino for their fight and attracted enthusiastic crowds, according to the *Tonopah Times*, which said the pair, "are having more interest shown by daily crowds than has been manifest since the Gans-Nelson contest of 1906. (The Gans-Nelson lightweight title fight was Tex Rickard's first promotional endeavor."

The second Dempsey-Sudenberg fight was another action-packed barnburner as Dempsey came out determined for a quick knockout – a pattern that he would follow throughout his career. The *Daily Bonanza* provided a round-by-round description:

> Round 1—Dempsey's mass attacks and Sudenberg's unpreparedness resulted in three floorings and one slip. Evidently, Dempsey's ambition to end the battle before his antagonist could recover his defense. Superior height and reach, together with Johnny's crouching position prevented return of blows. Uppercut to jaw set local man groggy. Jack swings twice to face, missing both, then left jab and right to face. Sudenberg takes count on right to jaw. Again takes count on right to body and right, left and right to jaw. Again downed on two to stomach. Sudenberg misses swing and is fought to ropes. Sudenberg lands to face as gong sounds.

Dempsey described the rest of the fight this way:

"He covered and made me chase him for the next five (rounds). By the sixth, that free lunch training table started to tell on me. He stretched me out three times in the seventh. For the rest of the fight, we just stood there and hit each other until we couldn't hold our hands up. It was called a draw and I think that's just what it was."

The *Daily Bonanza*, and some of the 1,100 fans weren't so sure:

Referee Minnick holds up right arms of both. Decision greeted with cheers and protests, some observers claiming that of the ten rounds eight were Dempsey's and one was drawn, but the referee based his decision on

Sudenberg's recovery of strength and has taking the offensive so strongly in the tenth.

The paper even printed a statement from referee J. H. Minnick justifying his decision to call the bout a draw. It read in part:

"Dempsey spent himself in five rounds, receiving much grandstand applause, but Sudenberg recuperated so rapidly and in the sixth to the finish grew stronger. In the ninth, Dempsey suffered a hard right to the stomach and weakness from there on, and if the limit would have permitted, he could not have endured the punishment three rounds more."

Jack Dempsey, right, and Johnny Sudenberg square off in a 1915 fight in Goldfield. It was declared a draw and Dempsey said he was carted back to the dugout cave in which he was staying in a wheelbarrow. *Colleen Rosencrantz Collection*

Jack Cuddy was a reporter at ringside and he reminisced about the bout in a 1939 story he wrote for United Press, which ran in the *Nevada State Journal*. Twenty-four years later, Cuddy's memory led to a few embellishments, but was mostly accurate.

"Jack always had that crushing right. He had it in 1915. He had it that night in '15 when he fought Johnny Sudenberg under the silvering Nevada stars in Tonopah –

in the terrific old Aerodrome (sic). That terrific right floored Sudenberg six times in the first two rounds (actually only three in the first round). But the tough Dutchman from Utah (Sudenberg was from Omaha, Neb.) kept picking himself off the canvas and fighting back—boring into Dempsey's innards until the welcome bell ended those historic 10 rounds. Dempsey won (the fight was actually a draw, though The Ring record book also lists it as a Dempsey win) but he sat there in his corner—a very sick light heavyweight—feeding imaginary fishes.

Only recently Dempsey told me, "that was the only fight I ever wanted to quit in. But I said to myself—if I quit now I'll never get anyplace in this business. And this business is the only business I know."

Dempsey and Sudenberg were each paid $100 for the fight, but the money wasn't with them for long. After patching up their cuts, they entered the Cobweb Saloon for a few beers, receiving cheers from the miners and others who had watched their fight.

"The bartender wouldn't take our money," Dempsey recalled. "But two other guys would."

"Suddenly, there was a strange silence in the joint. The bartender put up his hands. Johnny and I turned around. Two tough-looking guys had guns on us. They cleaned us and the others. Completely. I was broke again."

The two fighters decided it was time to get out of town. They spotted a handcar, unguarded on the tracks and headed north, ending up miles away at a place Dempsey called Miners Junction. It was likely Mina Junction, about 60 miles from Tonopah.

"I don't remember how far it was, but when we got there, we were completely pooped, punchy and starving."

They found a saloon and introduced themselves as prizefighters, offering to put on an exhibition if the patrons would pass the hat. It was not nearly as lucrative as their earlier bouts.

"We fought our bloody best for ten rounds and passed the hat. They chipped in $3.60. We had fought thirty awful minutes for a buck-eighty each. I could have begged that much in an hour."

Still broke and hungry, they jumped a train north to the tiny station of Wabuska in Lyon County and walked to the Teglia family farm, five miles west of Fort Churchill where they begged a job picking potatoes.

Roger Teglia, a longtime Reno resident, was a youngster at the time, but remembered the encounter well.

> "There was two fellows who came up to the ranch, wondering if we had any work for them to do. They were hitchhiking up to Virginia City. One of them happened to be Jack Dempsey. I guess he ran out of money so he walked from Wabuska clear over to our ranch. That's quite a few miles. He stayed almost a week and helped pick potatoes and I'd say he was quite a worker. We never knew that at the time that he was going to be a world champion prizefighter."

Dempsey and Sudenberg made their way to Reno, where Jack Thurm, who had promoted Dempsey's fight with Anamas Campbell, planned to match them in the main event of a card on July 27 at the Aerodome Arena for the "heavyweight championship of the west." The *Nevada State Journal* ran three stories promoting the bout, the third of which included a photo of Dempsey, who was rail-thin everywhere but his arms and shoulders.

> Everything is in readiness for the heavyweight fight to be staged by the Jockey Athletic Club in the new areodome arena on Fourth Street, just opposite the Nevada Packing House.
> Both Sudenberg and Dempsey have trained hard for this fight and are both in shape to put up the battle of their lives. Neither of them need introduction to the fight fans in Reno as they have both fought here before and have always finished on the winning end.

Both fighters were guaranteed $150 for the bout. But the fight never happened.

"It seemed too good to be true and it was," Dempsey recalled. "Johnny didn't show. Nobody else would box me. So I didn't get a nickel. I don't know why he ducked. He was a decent guy and he sure wasn't afraid of me. That I know from the thirty rounds of trying to scare him."

Broke, discouraged and disgusted with himself, Dempsey jumped a train and returned to Salt Lake City, figuring he could dig ditches for a living and at least be able to eat regularly.

Despite his discouragement, he wasn't done with boxing and he wasn't done with Sudenberg.

Jack Dempsey poses for a photograph in 1917, about the time he joined forces with manager Jack Kearns. *Colleen Rosencrantz Collection*

Coming of Age in Ely

4

Jack Dempsey's self-imposed exile from boxing was short-lived. After all, he had just turned 20 in June of 1915 and had been training himself to be a boxer for as long as he could remember. When he was just 11 years old, at the urging of his older brother Bernie who was also a prize-fighter, young Jack chewed pine pitch to strengthen his jaw. He also bathed his face and hands in beef brine to toughen the skin. It was a practice he continued for years. While he could dig ditches or wash dishes or work in the mines or push cattle, there was nothing he wanted more than to be a fighter. So after a few weeks, he was back at the gym in the back of Jackson's saloon in Salt Lake City.

It was there he met a Salt Lake man named Jack Price who offered to become his manager. Dempsey agreed and by December of 1915, he was back in the ring, fighting a four-round draw against Jack Downey and knocking out Two Round Gillian in the first round in Salt Lake City. In January of 1916, he fought a black fighter named Boston Bearcat and knocked him out in the first round. It was, perhaps, Dempsey's most impressive victory as the Bearcat had held his own against Sam Langford, considered one of the top heavyweights of the day.

Dempsey was honing his skills and his confidence was growing. He was ready to start venturing out of Utah again and the road led him back to Nevada and another matchup with Johnny Sudenberg. This one took place Feb. 5, 1916 at the Bijo Hall in Ely as an undercard fight, one of the fights held prior to the main event. It didn't last long and it didn't go over well in

Ely, not because of anything Dempsey did, but because of Sudenberg. The *Ely Record* reported: "The first preliminary was a disappointment. Jack Dempsey, a recent arrival in the district and manifestly a fighter, was matched against a long individual known as the 'Big Swede.' The Swede had evidently been looking upon the wine that is red or the beer that foameth. He was in no condition for a fight and a gentle tap from Dempsey sent him to the mat to stay."

The *White Pine News* was even less generous to Sudenberg:

> Announcer Lawrence made the statement that there would be two preliminaries, but this proved erroneous. The show was formally opened when two men stepped through the ropes, one a prize fighter and the other a human crustation (sic) of the lobster variety. Jack Dempsey came from Salt Lake some time ago and has since had difficulty in trying to get a match. … Jack Dempsey is a coming man in the prize ring and the Big Swede who was finally selected to meet him evidently had been imbibing a little too freely when he entered the ring. He tried to amuse the audience with what he evidently thought was funny gestures but Dempsey took a different view of it. He was there to fight and give the audience a run for their money. He evidently became disgusted with the Big Swede, as did everyone else, and Dempsey simply sent over what to him would be like a fly landing on his back, when the other gentleman dropped to the floor and remained there with his eyes wide open showing almost human intelligence until somebody finally cleared the ring for a bout.

Dempsey's victory via a second-round knockout would be the last of his memorable bouts with Sudenberg. Dempsey returned to Utah for fights with Jack Downey in Salt Lake and Cyril Kohn in Provo. Both fights were quick knockouts and Dempsey was ready for a little stiffer competition. He found it waiting for him in Ely.

On March 31, 1916, promoter Tom Chambers announced a 10-round main event matchup of Dempsey and Joe Bond, a veteran heavyweight who had just returned from Australia. Bond, who was from Tacoma, Wash., had also just broken up with his manager, Jack Kearns, a man that would play a key role in Dempsey's future.

"I had read about Bond," Dempsey recalled. "He was far and away the best man I had signed to face up to that time."

Bond apparently hadn't heard of Dempsey and sneered confidently at the skinny youngster when they entered the ring at the Bijo on the night of April 8. The large crowd got its money's worth as the bout went the distance and had plenty of action from the start. This time, Dempsey had the endurance to finish strong and there was no doubt as to the winner. The *Ely Record* said "when referee Smoot held Dempsey's hand aloft and declared him the winner, the cheering grew into a roar which was fairly deafening." The *White Pine News* called it "the best battle ever witnessed in the western country" and added "The eighth, ninth and tenth were clearly Dempsey's rounds and when all were taken into account, it could be said that Dempsey had five rounds, five were even and Bond had one."

Dempsey returned to Salt Lake a confident young man. He won a 10-round decision over Terry Keller in Ogden, then had quick knockouts against Dan Ketchell and George Christian in Price, Utah. By the end of May, both Dempsey and his manager felt he was ready for the big time. They pooled their money and hopped a train for New York.

They planned to find fights along the route to help pay their way, but soon discovered that while Dempsey might have made a name for himself in the west, he was unknown everywhere else and fights were nearly impossible to secure. He was turned away in Kansas City, St. Louis, Chicago and Cleveland. He and Price settled into a hotel in New York, but eventually had to move to the benches of Central Park because they were out of money for everything but gym fees.

Finally, in late June, Price was able to secure Dempsey a fight with Andre Anderson at Billy Gibson's Fairmont Club. The fight didn't start well for Dempsey. "He knocked me down a couple of times in the first three rounds. Then I lost count. In the fifth, he started to tire, probably exhausted from knocking me down. I gave him a real good pasting for the last five rounds." Dempsey won the "newspaper decision", which means a majority of the newspaper reporters present though he won. Among the writers was a young Damon Runyon, who would later become a great friend of Dempsey's. Dempsey and Price split $18 for the fight.

Two weeks later, Dempsey took on Wild Bert Kenny and again won the newspaper decision. This time, the payday was $28, $14 each for the fighter and his manager. "I could have sold the blood for $14," Dempsey said of what he called "one of the most brutal fights of my life."

Dempsey's work in the ring caught the attention of John "The Barber"

Reisler, a New York fight manager and gambler. Whether it was a homesick Price who sold him Dempsey's contract for $50 or it was Reisler who tricked Price into returning to Utah, Dempsey suddenly found himself being managed by "The Barber."

Reisler first proposed a match between Dempsey and Sam Langford, an experienced black fighter but Dempsey refused. Next, Reisler demanded Dempsey fight Gunboat Smith, another veteran fighter with vastly superior experience to Dempsey. Again, Dempsey refused. Finally, "The Barber" gave Dempsey no choice. He would fight John Lester Johnson or he would never fight again in New York – or anywhere else if Reisler had his way. Dempsey took the fight and also took the worst beating of his life. A body shot in the second round broke three ribs. Dempsey simply tried to survive the final eight rounds and somehow managed. The majority of writers gave the decision, rightfully Dempsey said, to Johnson. As he was getting his ribs taped up after the fight, Reisler gave him $35, saying their share was $85 each, but he was taking the $50 he'd given Price for Dempsey's contract out of Dempsey's share.

Angry, injured and discouraged, Dempsey went back on the rods and returned to Salt Lake City. He took a job in a copper mine to try to make ends meet while his ribs healed.

By late September, he felt well enough to take a fight with Young Hector in Salida, Colo., and scored a third-round knockout. A week late, he was back in Ely, preparing for a bout with Terry Keller. White Pine County was thrilled to have him back as evidenced by an October 1 front-page story in the *White Pine News*.

> Since the day when Joe Gans and Battling Nelson met in Goldfield and the eyes of all the world were then turned toward the great gold camp, not in search of the precious metal, but serious to learn who was the true champion, never has there been a battle staged in this country which has attracted more attention or which was of greater importance than the one which Promoter Tom Chambers has arranged for next Saturday night in the Bijo Hall.
>
> Jack Dempsey and Terry Keller will step through the ropes promptly at 9 o'clock to settle the question of which one is justly entitled to the title of "light heavyweight champion of the world."

The paper went on to describe Dempsey in glowing terms: "Jack Dempsey is undoubtedly the Bob Fitzsimmons of today. He is not only clever, but is a fighting demon. He is a glutton for punishment and the more that is administered to him, the faster he comes on."

The fight, however, couldn't live up to the hype of the advance story. In fact, the *White Pine News* took a distinctly different tone in its report on the fight, which Dempsey won by a 10-round decision. Referee C. W. Hicks' decision was described as, among other things, "no better than a can of spit", "a Pandora's box" and "a rose born to blush when showered with Mary Garden perfume."

Neither the writer of the article nor the crowd apparently wanted a Keller victory, but rather preferred the bout be called a draw. Despite their protests, the result went into the record book as a Dempsey win.

If it wasn't Dempsey's best performance, perhaps there were extenuating circumstances. He was, after all, still nursing broken ribs. But there might have been another distraction as well. Two days after the fight, he married a Salt Lake City "piano player" named Maxine Cates. The marriage was doomed from the start. Maxine was 15 years older than Dempsey and despite his pleas to settle down and provide him a family, she was more comfortable in her life in the underworld. They were divorced several months later, though Dempsey hadn't seen the last of Maxine, not by a long shot.

Jack Dempsey and his manager Doc Kearns, taken after they joined forces in 1917. *Colleen Rosencrantz Collection*

5

'Claimant to the World's Championship'

By the fall of 1918, Jack Dempsey was on a roll and on the trail of world heavyweight champion Jess Willard. Not that it had been an easy trip after his Ely fight with Terry Keller. Once again, there were plenty of bumps along the way: another trip to New York, an angry wife, a loss by knockout and days of no money, no food and little hope.

A few weeks after his wedding, Dempsey left Maxine in Salt Lake and returned to New York where "John the Barber" Reisler was waiting. Once again, Reisler demanded Dempsey take a fight with the more-experienced Sam Langford and once again Dempsey refused, saying he was no match for Langford at this point in his career. Dempsey's refusal ended his relationship with Reisler, who vowed to ruin his career.

Dempsey, flat broke again, rode the rods west, stopping in Kansas City for a 75-cents-a-day job as the sparring partner for Carl Morris, a big heavyweight who was training for a fight with Frank Moran. "The rules were simple," Dempsey recalled. "If I dumped him on his can, I'd be fired. I had a quarter in my pocket. I wasn't going to try to drop him. At least not then."

The job lasted only five days. Moran had hurt his hand in training and the bout was called off. Dempsey went back on the rods, leaving a note for Morris to forward his gloves, shoes and trunks to Martin's Saloon in Pueblo. Morris, a notorious skinflint, sent them C.O.D., and Dempsey had to beg for the 85 cents to claim them. He said later that of all the fighters he faced, Morris was the only one he ever truly disliked. Morris would feel Dempsey's wrath on more than one occasion.

In February of 1917 in Murray, Utah, Dempsey was knocked out in the first round by Fireman Jimmy Flynn. It was the only time in his career he was ever knocked out and rumors persisted for years that Dempsey threw the fight because he and his new wife, Maxine, were in desperate need of money. Dempsey denied the charge all his life and no evidence was ever produced to validate such a claim.

Dempsey did resort to working in a Seattle shipyard to make money, while his wife, 15 years his senior, stayed with her mother in Walla Walla. Then an urgent telegram from his mother informing him of the murder of his brother Bruce called Dempsey back to Salt Lake. He arrived a day late to attend the funeral.

While in Utah, he received a letter from a fight manager named Jack "Doc" Kearns. Kearns was flamboyant and fast-talking. He wore tailored suits, gold rings and a diamond stickpin. He liked to keep an eye on his fighters past and present, so he learned of Dempsey when he defeated Joe Bond, Kearns' former fighter, in Ely.

Kearns asked Dempsey in the letter if he was ready to start fighting again. Dempsey immediately wrote back that he was available and Kearns, in response, sent him a train ticket to Oakland and a $5 bill. It was the start of one of the most remarkable partnerships in the history of boxing.

Dempsey fought Willie Meehan in San Francisco in his first bout with Kearns as his manager and settled for a draw. He was paid $250 for the fight and his days of riding the rods were over. He was fighting frequently and having success – including a long string of first-round knockouts – and before long, Kearns starting promoting Dempsey as the top challenger to champion Jess Willard.

In July of 1918, Dempsey knocked out Fred Fulton, the No. 1-contender for the world title, in 18 seconds of the first round in Harrison, N.J. It not only made him the top contender for Jess Willard's title, but the $5,000 payday also allowed him to buy his mother a house, something Dempsey called "the proudest day of my life."

In September of 1918, the *Nevada State Journal* reported a bout between Dempsey and Jack Moran was planned for Sept. 14 at Moana Springs. From the start of the year, Dempsey had won 14 of 15 fights and taken a no decision in the other. Of those 14 wins, 13 were by knockout and nine were first-round knockouts. But the night before his Reno bout, Dempsey lost a four-round decision to Willie Meehan in San Francisco, a fight that raised $18,000 for the Navy Relief Fund.

Kearns immediately went into spin control, sending a telegram to the

Reno newspapers through promoter Dem Gay claiming the referee was tricked into a poor decision. The telegram read: "Dempsey had Meehan on the floor and almost out in the second round. He beat him badly in every round. Meehan worked a clever trick when he lifted his own hand after the last round and (referee Eddie) Graney fell for the trick. The decision was almost as unpopular as the decision Wyatt Earp rendered in the Fitzsimmons-Sharkey bout. A draw would have been giving Dempsey the worst of it."

Kearns was referring to the 1896 heavyweight bout in San Francisco between Bob Fitzsimmons and Tom Sharkey in which Earp, the famous lawman, served as the referee. Fitzsimmons battered Sharkey throughout the bout and had him on the verge of a knock-out, but after what appeared to be a solid combination, Earp declared Fitzsimmons had fouled Sharkey, disqualifying Fitzsimmons. Many believe Earp was involved with gamblers who had bet on Sharkey.

Dempsey felt he had lost to Meehan. In his 1959 autobiography, Dempsey said Meehan "had slapped me around the ring."

Jack Moran had arrived in Reno a day earlier and sparred three rounds at Moana Springs with a University of Nevada boxer named Wilson. Moran assured reporters he was there to give Dempsey a fight. "My boy is out to win if he can," promoter Dem Gay told reporters. "The contest will be no exhibition, but a fight."

Later in the day, Moran put on an exhibition of "fancy diving" at the pool at Moana Springs. That exhibition certainly lasted longer than the fight itself. As the *Journal* reported:

> Jack Dempsey was in a hurry to finish things last night at Moana Pavilion in his bout with Jack Moran and finished his opponent in one minute and thirty seconds. The less experienced Moran was willing enough, but he could do nothing with the world's championship claimant. He was floored early for the count of nine and when he came back he was sent down and out for keeps.

Dempsey was back in form and on his way to a title shot with Jess Willard.

Champion Jess Willard tries to hold off Jack Dempsey in their championship fight in Toledo, Ohio, July 4, 1919. Dempsey won when Willard couldn't answer the bell for the fourth round. *Colleen Rosencrantz Collection*

6
Triumph in Toledo

I t took more than a year – and the help of a former Nevada resident – for Jack Dempsey to get Jess Willard to agree to a bout after Dempsey had become the No. 1 contender. For one thing, Willard didn't think much of Dempsey. For another, he liked Jack Kearns even less. But Willard also loved money and when fight promoter Tex Rickard, the former Goldfield saloon owner, guaranteed Willard $100,000 to defend his title, Willard agreed and gave Rickard the rights to select his opponent.

Rickard, who had promoted the Gans-Nelson fight in Goldfield in 1906 and the Jack Johnson-Jim Jeffries fight in Reno in 1910 for the heavyweight championship of the world, set about finding the right opponent for the massive Willard, who stood 6-feet-6 inches tall and weighed 250 pounds. Rickard knew he was taking a gamble because boxing was at a low point, mainly because of Willard's inactivity. After knocking out Johnson in Havana, Cuba in 1915 to win the title, Willard fought only twice in 1916, not at all in 1917 and only twice in exhibitions in 1918.

So Rickard was not only looking for a fighter who could effectively challenge Willard, but one who could excite the public about boxing again. After the Johnson-Jeffries fight and the racial riots and strife it produced following Johnson's victory, Rickard vowed he would never promote another interracial boxing match. That eliminated black contenders such as Sam Langford and Harry Wills. Veteran fighters including Bill Brennan, Gunboat Smith and Fred Fulton were also eliminated by Rickard for various reasons.

The only logical choice was Dempsey and Rickard arranged a meeting with Kearns and Dempsey at his office in New York City. The old gambler was reluctant because of Dempsey's size, 6-foot-1 and 180 pounds. "Every-time I look at you, you look smaller," he told Dempsey. "I'm afraid if I put you in the ring with Willard, you'll get killed. I'm afraid Willard will kill you."

Rickard, after all, knew Willard's history.

Like Dempsey, Willard had fought in Reno in the past. On July 4, 1913 at Moana Springs, he faced Al Williams, a heavyweight with a pretty fair reputation on the coast. Big crowds attended Willard's training camp with many Reno residents traveling by trolley to the Moana Springs site south of town.

The 205-pound William was no pushover, but simply couldn't get inside the taller and heavier Willard, who used his superior reach to his advantage. Willard scored an eighth-round knockout after battering William throughout the fight.

In his very next fight, a month later in Vernon, Calif., Willard knocked out Bull Young in the 11th round with a right uppercut that drove the base of Young's jaw into his brain. The Wyoming fighter died in a Los Angeles Hospital the next day.

Two years later in Havana, Willard pounded Jack Johnson to win the title, but it was the memory of the Young fight that had Rickard fearful of matching Dempsey against Willard.

Knowing he had no other real options, Rickard made the fight.

There was much haggling over how much Dempsey was to be paid. Kearns demanded $50,000 for the challenger, which Rickard refused. For one thing, there was the fear Willard might kill Dempsey. Secondly, Dempsey was still an unproven fighter in Rickard's opinion. Rickard thought $10,000 was a fair purse for the challenger. Finally, the decision was thrown open to a group of sportswriters, including Damon Runyon, the man who gave Dempsey the nickname "the Manassa Mauler." They agreed Dempsey should be paid $27,500 for the bout.

The next challenge was selecting a location for the fight. New York was out of the picture. The Frawley Law of 1911, permitted fights of up to 10 rounds in New York, but prohibited official decisions. That is why Dempsey's earlier New York fights relied on the newspaper decisions because no official decisions were allowed. The most obvious choice, particularly to New York sportswriter Al Spink, was Reno. In fact, Spink, who founded *The Sporting News*, felt Reno was the only place to stage the bout, as he detailed in a story in the March 10, 1919 edition of the *Reno Evening Gazette*, under the headline

"Al Spink Declares Willard-Dempsey Coming Here."

Rickard is a wise gambler. He plays no game without knowing it thoroughly. When he signed up Willard and Dempsey, it is a cinch he had an ace up his sleeve. That ace is Reno. There is no other place in America that will produce a gate of $270,775. That is the amount taken in when Johnson and Jeffries, under the management of Rickard, fought there.

A few weeks before Rickard closed with Willard and Dempsey, someone went to work trying to get a boxing bill through the Nevada Legislature. After the Johnson-Jeffries fight in Nevada, the legislature of that state passed a law allowing only ten-round fights. Two years ago, an effort was made to obtain a twenty-five round fight law in Nevada, which failed, but a few weeks ago, that sort of a law was passed.

A day or two later, the governor vetoed the bill, but now it has passed over his veto.

In the meantime, just to wake up the people of Nevada to "the good thing that is liable to get away from them," Rickard or his agents are sending out telegrams from various places, saying he prefers Chicago, New York, Halifax and various other places where there are not a chance on earth of bringing off a battle for the heavyweight championship.

In the meanwhile, Rickard's friends in Nevada, and he has a lot of them there, are working and at the proper time you will hear that the coast is clear and that Rickard is making arrangements to build a big arena in Reno, one that will make the Johnson-Jeffries arena look like thirty cents. There is every reason in the world why Rickard should take the fight to Reno.

A week later, Spink's confidence in Reno was starting to wane and he surmised Rickard hadn't announced the bout there because he was still waiting to receive "a bonus" from the city.

At the same time, Reno wasn't the only Nevada city said to be in pursuit of the fight. Tonopah also placed a bid. In addition, the Elko newspaper, after seeing Tonopah's effort, lamented that Elko should also make a bid because its rodeo arena was far superior a site than anything Tonopah could offer.

Ultimately, Rickard considered several locations for the fight, but finally decided Toledo, Ohio. Though a mid-sized town of about 140,000, Toledo was a hub of both rail and sea traffic. At least 10 railroad companies and six Great Lakes steamship companies served the city, providing easy access for fight fans from the large metropolitan areas of the East and upper Midwest. Contracts with the City of Toledo were signed May 7, 1919, with Rickard agreeing that 7 percent of the gate would go into a fund for the poor of Toledo.

The fight was set for July 4 at Bayview Park, a site on the north side of Toledo overlooking Maumee Bay. Rickard immediately secured the services of San Francisco contractor James P. McLaughlin to construct an open-air arena with seating for 80,000. It was McLaughlin who had built the arena in Reno for the Johnson-Jeffries fight and the stadium was designed in much the same manner with one notable exception – Rickard, fearful of gate crashers like those he experienced in Reno, ordered that there be only one entrance to the stadium. The final cost for the stadium, which consisted of two million feet of lumber, was $150,000. It was sold a week after the fight to the American House Wrecking Company for $25,000.

Toledo had a reputation at the time as a wide-open town where prohibition was routinely ignored. As the fight approached, its population expanded significantly. Both fighters set up training camp on the shores of Maumee Bay. An estimated 600 sports writers from around the country flocked to town. Among them were luminaries such as Bat Masterson, the former frontier lawman turned sportswriter for the *New York Morning Telegraph*; Ring Lardner of the *New York World*; Bill McGeehan and Grantland Rice of the *New York Tribune* and Damon Runyon of the *New York American*. Several papers hired fighters to provide their coverage, including the *Chicago Observer*, which obtained the services of Battling Nelson, the middleweight of Goldfield fame.

Nelson was low on funds and set up a tent at Dempsey's training camp. Never known for his good personal hygiene, Nelson's actions in the early-morning hours on the day of the fight are a story in themselves and nobody told the story better than Dempsey.

> It was the hottest July 4 I could remember. Some
> said it was 100 in the shade; others said 110. All I know
> is the resin boiled out of the bleacher seats and before
> the fight began, they were selling hot "ice water" for a

dollar a glass. They had run out of lemonade, but it wasn't much good anyway. Bat Nelson had gotten up early that morning and decided to take a bath in honor of the occasion. He looked around the grounds and found a nice big hogshead filled with what he though was water. He scrounged some soap and took a nice bath in it. It was the lemonade (to be sold at the concession stands during the fight).

Back in Nevada, Reno was in the midst of a massive celebration of its own. With the end of World War I, city leaders decided to hold a rodeo and western carnival, complete with parades, horse races and all sorts of activities. At the same time, the Dempsey-Willard fight was big news in Reno as well. In fact, organizers made a point to schedule the parade prior to the start of the fight and the rodeo after the conclusion of the fight. Here is how the *Nevada State Journal* described the scene:

> Reno is all aglow today for one of the biggest celebrations in its history. The streets are thronged with crowds of people coming from all parts of Nevada and from adjoining states. The hotels are packed to capacity and hundreds are awaiting for accommodations. The buildings, both business and residential, are fully decorated with flags. And the plans for the day's celebrations are complete and ready for execution at the fixed hours.
>
> The program for today is as follows: 12:30, parade of Round-Up contestants; 1:00, Willard-Dempsey fight by rounds in front of Journal office over direct wire to the paper; 2:00, Nevada Round-Up at state fair grounds…

Both the *Journal* and *Reno Evening Gazette* carried wire service previews of the bout and the general consensus was that Willard was the heavy favorite. However, both papers did carry stories saying the betting action by the gamblers in attendance was "mostly even." The two fighters issued statements to The Associated Press. "I believe that I am in perfect shape and confident that I shall successfully defend the championship," Willard said. "If it should prove that I am wrong, I shall stand up like a man and admit the superior boxing ability of my opponent without quibble, excuse or alibi." Said Dempsey: "That I have real confidence in my ability to take the title away from Willard is to be believed. I have never yet met a man I feared. They all look alike to me and unless Willard is the superman claimed by his supporters I will knock him out in a hurry."

One person who didn't believe Dempsey was his own father, who made the trip from Utah to watch the fight. Hyrum Dempsey told sportswriters that while his son was a good boy, Willard was just too big and would knock his son out in the fourth round.

Finally, it was fight time. Dempsey was first into the ring. He was listed at 188 pounds, though he said he had stuffed himself with bananas for the weigh-in and actually weighed about 180. He had shaved the sides of his head and as he entered the ring, he was wearing only an old cardigan over his shoulders instead of a robe. He stood in the heat for what seemed an eternity as Willard made him wait. At last the champion made his way to the ring.

Willard weighed 250 pounds, and despite assurances from Kearns that Willard was fat and out of shape, Dempsey quickly saw otherwise. "He came into the ring like a moving mountain, dropped his robe and held up his arms to the cheering crowd. I thought I was going to get sick to my stomach," Dempsey recalled. "Kearns had kept telling me what a bum Willard was—big, fat, no good. Now as I looked up the wall of his back, I could see he was in terrific shape. The way he was holding up his arms made his fists seem twice as high in the air as I was tall. The muscle stood out on his back. I looked at all six feet six and 250 pounds of him and I said to myself, 'This guy's liable to kill me.'"

Dempsey couldn't look up at Willard and instead set his gaze on the champion's midsection. As one report described the scene, "The mood of the challenger was plainly thoughtful, and more than one ring-side gazer whispered: 'He's licked right now.'"

In a strange twist, the bell was not working at the start of the fight. Workers repairing the canvas in the ring had inadvertently slipped a guy rope between the clapper and the bell, so a whistle had to be used to start the bout. It started slowly, unusual for Dempsey whose typical pattern was to rush across the ring and swarm his opponent. Instead, he showed the much-larger champion plenty of respect.

Willard flicked two left jabs into Dempsey's face. Dempsey missed a swing. They clinched and as he slipped from it, Dempsey hit Willard with three quick body blows. Again they clinched and this time Willard broke free with a left to the head and another to the body. About a minute had gone by and those blows from Willard seemed to ignite Dempsey. A jarring left to the ribs was followed by a right and then another left to the body. "The almost superhuman power of the punches were immediately apparent," wrote one reporter. They became even more apparent with the next series of blows from the challenger. Dempsey slipped inside and landed a left to Willard's jaw. This was followed by a right and left to the body, another right to the head and then "a perfect left hook" to the side of Willard's face. It shattered the champion's cheekbone and sent him sprawling to the canvas.

Willard was up at the count of six, but only for an instant. In this era, fighters did not have to go to a neutral corner after a knockout and could stand above their fallen opponent, which is exactly what Dempsey did. As soon as Willard rose, another left hook sent him back to the canvas. It also knocked out six of the champion's teeth. Blood poured from his mouth, covering Dempsey as they clinched. Again Willard rose only to be met with another flurry of punches from Dempsey. Down again, and again, and again, and again. Seven knockdowns in all, the last coming from a series of body blows.

Referee Ollie Pecord counted the dazed Willard out. Kearns climbed through the ropes and shouted, "Jack, you're the champ." Kearns was ecstatic because he had placed a $10,000 bet at 10-to-1 odds that Dempsey would score a first-round knockout. He pointed Dempsey toward his dressing room and the challenger left the ring.

He was almost to his dressing room when he heard Kearns' frantic shouts to get back into the ring. The fight was not over. The whistle to end the round had come before the referee had finished counting Willard out and the fight was still on. Because of the crowd noise, no one heard the whistle.

Newspaper reports described it this way: "Dempsey thought the referee had announced him winner and actually left the ring. But he was called back and the butchery continued for two rounds more when Jess, sitting in his corner with a bewildered look on his swollen countenance, failed to respond to the gong for the fourth round."

Searching for an analogy to describe the fight, The Associated Press writer at ringside referred to the Johnson-Jeffries fight of 1910 in Reno. "(Willard) received in nine minutes of fighting far more punishment than did Jeffries a the hands of Jack Johnson in their 15-round bout at Reno."

As he had promised, Willard made no alibi for his defeat and praised the new champion. "Dempsey is a remarkable hitter. It was the first time that I had ever been knocked off my feet. I have sent many boxers home in the same bruised condition that I am now in and now I know how they feel. I sincerely wish Dempsey all the luck possible and hope that he garners in the riches that go with the championship. I have had my fling at the title."

Dempsey, too, was gracious.

"Willard is a game fellow. I never handed out more punishment to anyone and have him come right back for more as Willard did today."

Dempsey's first request after winning was that a telegram be sent to his
mother in Salt Lake City. It read simply: "Your boy made good. Knocked the
big fellow out in three rounds."

It was official. Jack Dempsey was heavyweight champion of the world.

On July 20, the *Nevada State Journal* reported that after a meeting of
miners and operators of the Willard mining district – so named after Willard
had defeated Jack Johnson for the title – voted to change its name to the Lor-
ing District.

Jess Willard's star was fading as Jack Dempsey's turned bright.

7

Trouble From a Wells
Dance Hall

A day after winning the world's heavyweight championship, Jack Dempsey left Toledo for a week on stage in Cincinnati. It had become a tradition for the heavyweight champion to perform on Vaudeville and in the movies and Doc Kearns – never one to let an opportunity for money to slip past – capitalized at every turn. When the week in Cincinnati was completed, Dempsey and Kearns set up a base in Chicago where Kearns was reported to be busy "talking with promoters and agents of theatrical and circus concerns, anxious to have Dempsey sign contracts for exhibitions." Kearns completed much of the business in one day and on the night of July 13, he and Dempsey headed for the West Coast.

On July 17, they arrived in Los Angeles, where Dempsey was the guest of honor at a luncheon of sports writers and local sportsmen (gamblers). After the luncheon, he attended a Coast League baseball game and was presented to the crowd from home plate. Later that night, he and Kearns left for San Francisco where they spent a few days living the high life in their old stomping grounds. The *San Francisco Chronicle* observed Dempsey and his ever-present entourage of ex-fighters, women and hangers-on living it up at a number of San Francisco bars and cafes. "Dempsey bought all the drinks and enjoyed plenty of the 4.5 percent beer himself," the paper reported.

As the champion later recalled, he was free as a bird, having been divorced from Maxine months before. The world opened up to Dempsey and he freely accepted all the perks of being the world champion.

After a couple of days in the Bay Area, Dempsey headed for Salt Lake City to visit his mother. No doubt he passed through northern Nevada on his way, though if he stopped in the Silver State, it wasn't documented. If he passed through Wells in Elko County, it was within only a few feet of Maxine, who, after the divorce, had taken a job in a "dance hall" owned by a woman named Tommy Wilson. The fact that Maxine was a prostitute was not much of a secret. Dempsey said later that he still loved Maxine even after the divorce and would have reconciled with her if she had been willing to give up her life in the underworld and settle down. If he stopped in Wells, it was a brief visit, though there is some circumstantial evidence that he did. Maxine later said she had become jealous when she heard that Tommy Wilson traveled east with Dempsey after he became champion. She later learned it was not true, though her jealousy and reaction to the rumor ignited a firestorm she could not put out.

On July 21, Dempsey was at his mother's home in Utah for a short visit. The *Nevada State Journal* ran this story from the wire service:

> SALT LAKE CITY, July 21.—Jack Dempsey, champion heavyweight pugilist, spent today with his mother, the first day at home for him since last winter.
>
> "This is the first real relaxation I have had since beginning training," Dempsey told the few callers who were allowed to pass a manager and several brothers in order to see him. Dempsey said that he had not signed any contracts for vaudeville or for future boxing contests, but that he is likely to go with a circus or on a vaudeville circuit shortly.
>
> Referring to the possibility of a fight with Willie Meehan, Dempsey declared he was willing to box with the California man if the people demanded it. He intimated that Carpentier would be his next opponent.
>
> After a few days here with his mother, Dempsey will go to Chicago, he said today.
>
> Dempsey was to appear publicly tonight in aid of the Salvation Army home service drive.

For the next several months, Dempsey set about making money – lots of money. Back in Chicago, he joined a vaudeville troupe for $10,000 a week, paid in advance. The show went broke after seven weeks, but Dempsey – and, of course, Kearns – had their money. Dempsey then joined up with the

Sells-Floto Circus Troupe and spent several months with them for about $2,500 a week. But it was Hollywood that beckoned and Dempsey soon made his way to Southern California and the motion picture business. In December of 1919, he rented a home in the Silver Lake district of Los Angeles, and soon signed a contract with Pathé Studios to star in a serial called *Daredevil Jack*. He received $10,000 up front and $1,000 a week. His friends included the biggest stars of the day, including Douglas Fairbanks, Rudolph Valentino, Tom Mix and Charlie Chaplin.

He seemed to be on top of the world and then, on January 23, 1920, a letter to the editor appeared in the *San Francisco Chronicle* and turned Dempsey's world upside down. The headline read: "Dempsey Slacker, Says Divorced Wife/She Claims to Have the Proofs/Dares Champion to Deny Her Charges." The letter writer – or at least the name that appeared on the letter – was Maxine Dempsey.

In the letter, Maxine accused Dempsey and Doc Kearns of conspiring to have Dempsey granted 4-A status to avoid service in The Great War. Not only had Dempsey never supported her, she wrote, but she had supported him with money she earned working in a dancehall. She also wrote that her proof existed in letters from Dempsey's own hand and she would make these letters available at an appropriate time."

If the letter was meant to send shockwaves through the sports world, it certainly did and smack in the middle of the storm was the tiny town of Wells, Nevada. Within a day of the letter's publication, telegrams began pouring in for Maxine Dempsey, "with such rapidity that she would have been compelled to employ an army of stenographers had she attempted to answer all of them," the weekly *Nevada State Herald* reported in a front page story on Jan. 30, 1920.

Soon after the telegrams came the writers, and others, dispatched from all around the country. The *Herald* provided the details under the headline "Writers come here for big sensation; meet disappointment."

> For several days, up to Monday, Wells was the center-piece of the thoughts of thousands of people of the United States and the name of the town was quoted in dispatches and newspapers from Maine to San Francisco. Newspaper men and correspondents from all over the coast were arriving on every train, and among them were some mysterious personages, whose mission they kept to themselves.

Many people believe some of the visitors were employed by one Jack Dempsey to watch his divorced wife, Maxine Dempsey. …

Jack Dempsey's first wife, Maxine Cates, left, poses with Dempsey's sister, Florence at the family home in Salt Lake City. *Colleen Rosencrantz Collection*

Nearly every train during last Friday, Saturday and Sunday brought one or more writers, each bent on securing the "exclusive" story of the precious possessions of Mrs. Dempsey. But all of them went away with about as much information of a reliable nature as they possessed when they arrived.

The reason for the writers' disappointment was that Maxine had already left town, accompanied by three of her fellow dance hall residents, who she referred to as her bodyguards. A dispatch said she had gone to Ogden, Utah and checked into the Healy Hotel using the name of Miss Maida Rice. It was reported she had suffered a nervous breakdown and was under a doctor's care and confined to her bed.

Kearns and Dempsey weren't about to let Maxine's charges go unchallenged. On the same day her letter appeared in the San Francisco Chronicle, Dempsey sent a telegram to Major A.J. Drexel Biddle, president of the army, navy and civilian boxing board in New York City asking for a formal investigation. In the telegram, Dempsey pointed out that the board had issued him a license just prior to his match with Jess Willard that certified that he had "a clean and honorable record as a professional boxer and that he had the full sanction and approval of the board. Dempsey received License No. 2, the first card going to Willard, who was then champion."

The U.S. Attorney's office in San Francisco also investigated the case at the insistence of California American Legion posts, and within 10 days, decided to bring charges against both Dempsey and Kearns. This decision came despite another letter from Maxine, where she retracted her original claims. On Feb. 4, she sent a notarized statement to the Chronicle that started: "Jack Dempsey is not a slacker."

But the wheels were already in motion and the case moved ahead. The lead prosecutor on the case was Charles W. Thomas, a former adjutant-general of the California National Guard. He took his case to a grand jury and on Feb. 24, 1920, an indictment was handed up charging Dempsey and Kearns with conspiracy to avoid the draft.

Dempsey and his handlers (by now, Rickard and several Hollywood executives were also involved) set out to find help, an endeavor that took them all the way to the White House and Joe Tumulty, a chief advisor of President Woodrow Wilson. While Wilson was not involved in the discussions, Dempsey's team left the White House with a letter of introduction written to San Francisco lawyer Gavin McNab. McNab, a lawyer of several Hollywood stars including silent-screen star Mary Pickford, agreed to take the case for a fee of $75,000. McNab was in Reno in early June, just days before the start of the Dempsey trial, to help prepare a presentation to the Nevada Supreme Court concerning Pickford's divorce from Owen Moore, one of Nevada's first high-profile divorce cases. In Reno, McNab met with lawyer Patrick McCarran, the future U.S. Senator, who argued the case before the state Supreme Court because McNab had to be in San Francisco for Dempsey's trial.

Proceedings in San Francisco started on June 8 with Judge Maurice J. Dooling presiding. The courtroom was packed, primarily with spectators wearing American Legion buttons. In addition, several army officers were also in attendance, one of them speaking a greeting to the prosecutor, addressing him as "Colonel Thomas." McNab, meanwhile, had brought in Dempsey's parents, who sat side by side throughout the trial despite the fact that they were separated and in the process of getting a divorce. Dempsey's brother, Bernie, suffering from lung disease, was there, as was his sister Effie Clarkson, a widow in frail health.

A confident Thomas had hinted to reporters that he had 35 letters from Dempsey to Maxine that would prove Dempsey's guilt. The contents of the letters would, he said, be revealed in due time. On the first day of the trial, Thomas called Rudolph Goodman, a notary public from Chicago, who testified he was present when Dempsey filled out his selective service questionnaire and had helped fill it out. He said while he asked Dempsey the questions, it was Kearns who answered them. On the questionnaire, Dempsey listed his wife, mother, father and sister as his dependent. Thomas' next two witnesses, both from Salt Lake City, were called to illustrate that both Dempsey's father, Hyrum, and Dempsey's sister, Effie, had earned income of their own in 1917, Hyrum $472 and Effie $250. By the end of the first day, newspaper men were in agreement it had been a bad day for Dempsey.

The second day, however, the prosecution's case hit a significant roadblock. Thomas called Maxine, who was conspicuously absent from the courtroom on day 1, to the witness stand and moved to put the 35 letters into evidence. McNabb immediately objected, saying the introduction of the letters would be in violation of the doctrine that neither party in a marriage can testify against the other. Judge Dooling ruled in McNabb's favor despite heated objections from Thomas, who said the letters were central to the issue of Dempsey's conspiracy to avoid service. Dooling said he would consider the issue overnight and make a final ruling the next day. In the meantime, Thomas should continue his case.

Thomas called several of Maxine's friends as witnesses, trying to establish that Dempsey had not supported Maxine. The women told of working with Maxine at various whorehouses from Wells, Nevada to Cairo, Illinois. All the witnesses testified that Dempsey had never sent his wife a dime.

On the third day, Maxine finally took the stand and when Thomas tried to introduce one of the letters, Dooling read it and then ruled, without comment, that it could not be admitted as evidence. He also announced, "there would be no general rule as to what was non-confidential matter and the questions which it gives rise to will be settled as they arise." With the letters essentially barred, Maxine testified about her travels in the underworld, including stops in Pasco, Spokane and Yakima, Washington; Cairo Ill., Salida, Colo., and Salt Lake City. She also testified that she and Dempsey had come to San Francisco together and that Dempsey "had once struck her on the jaw because she did not bring him enough money to satisfy him." At this testimony, Dempsey became visibly upset in the courtroom and started to rise before being calmed by his brother and McNab.

In cross-examination, Maxine admitted she signed the draft questionnaire of her husband, attesting to her dependence upon him. She also admitted that Dempsey had sent her money. McNab produced witnesses from the Western Union office in Salt Lake City, who brought along receipts and testified that Maxine was a frequent visitor to their office to pick up money. R.W. Burton, a cashier in the office, testified that after the Fulton fight, Dempsey had wired $200 to Maxine, who cracked "that Fulton must have hit Jack hard to jar him loose from $200."

McNab also hammered Maxine on why she had kept the letters and the nature of her intentions. By the end of his cross-examination, it was clear Maxine had done so for her own personal gain.

Maxine was the final government witness, so on the fourth day, McNab opened the defense, calling Dempsey's mother to the stand. Soft-spoken and composed, Celia Dempsey testified how her son had supported the family, sending money whenever he could. After winning the championship from Willard, Dempsey had returned to Salt Lake and bought the family a $20,000 home. "We wouldn't have had anything (without him)," she said.

By the time Dempsey took the stand on Monday, June 15, the momentum was clearly in his favor. As a witness, he was matter-of-fact and composed as John Preston, one of McNab's co-counsels, walked him through a series of questions that refuted all of Maxine's charges against him. First, he compared Dempsey's earnings in 1917 with those of 1918. They were about the same – $4,000 – despite the fact that Dempsey had fought 22 times in 1918 and 13 times in 1917. When asked why the disparity, Dempsey replied, "I did most of my 1918 fighting for charity." Indeed, he had helped raise more than $330,000 for the war effort.

Dempsey denied the charge that he had struck his wife and testified at length about how he had begged her to make a home in Salt Lake City where they could start a family. Instead, he said, she decided to return to life in the underworld.

Finally, Dempsey testified that he had planned to enlist in the service and was in the process of doing in October of 1918 when Navy secretary Josephus Daniels ordered enlistments stopped. The last defense witness was Navy Lieutenant John F. Kennedy (no relation to the future president) who testified that Dempsey had, indeed, tried to enlist after putting on a boxing exhibition at Great Lakes Naval Training Station. In cross-examination, Thomas made a blunder when he asked Kennedy about his own overseas service. When Kennedy said he had not seen action, Thomas then called him "a bit of a slacker," causing at least one juror to gasp in surprise.

A confident McNab said there was no need for a summation. Thomas also declined a closing statement and the jurors received their instructions from Dooling. They deliberated for seven minutes before returning a verdict: not guilty.

An angry Maxine announced she was heading for Yakima, Washington to live temporarily with her mother, but that she would see the letters published. (They never were.)

Dempsey was elated: "All I can tell you is that right now I'm the happiest boy in the world."

8

A Bid from Broken Hills

Despite being cleared in his slacker trial, Jack Dempsey heard the whispers and catcalls of a largely unforgiving public and it pained him deeply for the rest of his life. In his 1959 autobiography, he wrote: "With the end of the war I hoped the matter was ended. It wasn't of course. It never will be, really, in my own heart. … I fought a Frenchman before an American audience and was booed. I fought an Argentinian before my countrymen and was booed. … It always dug deep and hurt terribly."

Two people who saw a way to take advantage of Dempsey's unpopularity (in a financial way, of course) were Tex Rickard and Jack Kearns. They saw the perfect hero to Dempsey's villain in the person of Georges Carpentier, a highly-decorated French war hero and the light heavyweight champion of the world. While talk of such a matchup was going on as early as 1919, serious talks didn't begin until late 1920.

In his climb to the championship, Dempsey had fought, and flattened, all the top heavyweights. He made two title defenses in 1920, scoring a third-round knockout over his old friend Billy Miske at Benton Harbor, Mich., on Sept. 6 and taking a 12-round knockout over Bill Brennan at Madison Square Garden in New York City on Dec. 14. The Brennan fight had been much closer than most, particularly Kearns and Rickard, expected. Dempsey had been hurt early in the fight and before scoring the decisive knockout, Brennan had turned his ear into a bloody mess, or as the great sportswriter Grantland Rice described it, "a cross between a veal cutlet and a bloody sponge." Dempsey was still champion, but perhaps, just perhaps, he was beatable.

The time was ripe for the Carpentier fight and Kearns, who didn't particularly like or trust Rickard – a feeling that was more than mutual – wanted to promote the fight himself. He guaranteed Carpentier's manager, Francois Deschamps, $200,000, for the bout. He soon found out, however, his plan for a grand event in London or another European site wasn't financially feasible. In addition, Kearns didn't have $200,000, and he only knew one person in the boxing game who could raise it and promote the fight in the manner Kearns envisioned – Tex Rickard. Kearns just didn't want Rickard to know that. He ran a scam on the old gambler. Kearns made it known he had a $500,000 offer from interests in Cuba to hold the bout in Havana. In November of 1920, Kearns met two Cuban businessmen for lunch at the Hotel Claridge, which happened to be Rickard's regular dining spot. He introduced Rickard to the men and told him of their $500,000 offer. Rickard fell for the bait and rushed to find financial backing for a domestic fight. It was weeks later when he learned the two Cuban businessmen were actually waiters from the hotel that Kearns had outfitted with new suits and $5 cigars.

When the contracts for Dempsey-Carpentier were signed, Dempsey was guaranteed $300,000 and 25 percent of the film rights and Carpentier was guaranteed $200,000 and the same percentage from the films. The press labeled it "the Battle of the Century." It would be, financially, the biggest prizefight in history – if they could just pull it off.

The contracts signed, Rickard spent the early months of 1921 searching for a site to hold the fight and offers came in from a diverse group of places – London, England; Cumberland, Maryland; Hollywood, California; and Broken Hills, Nevada.

Broken Hills, a mining camp located 125 miles east of Reno (about 15 miles northeast of present-day Gabbs), was born in 1913 after James Stratford and Joseph Arthur discovered a deposit of silver-lead ore. In its heyday, the camp had a few hundred residents, a hotel, saloon, stores and a school. But it had money – or the offer of money, at least. The March 30, 1921 edition of *The Fallon Standard* reported it this way:

> Broken Hills has entered the list of aspiring communities in the country making a bid for the Dempsey-Carpentier fight. Eight hundred thousand dollars constituted the purse in prospect from the partisans of the state's newest mining camp. This method has been adopted to bring Broken Hills into the limelight.
>
> In the old days, a mining camp was never deemed

of much account until it became possessed of a cemetery well filled with men with their feet encased in high topped leather footwear while nowadays mining camps attain prominence by championship boxing bouts.

Dr. W. E. Harrison, A. F. Branch and others interested in Broken Hills guarantee the eight hundred thousand. When asked yesterday if failure to attract a crowd wouldn't jeopardize their personal holdings, both replied with commendable nonchalance "what's money anyhow in these days when it costs half as much as the fight purse to prospect to outfit a Piute squaw for a matrimonial venture."

Branch not only had mining interests in Broken Hills, but the Cal-Neva Oil Company was drilling on his farm near Fallon amidst a reported oil boom in the Lahontan Valley that had drawn speculators from around the country.

It is not know if Rickard, who had once operated a saloon in Rawhide, just across the valley from the Broken Hills, gave the Nevada site any serious consideration. If anyone could promote a fight in the Nevada desert, Rickard was the man. He'd proven it in 1906 with the Gans-Nelson championship bout in Goldfield and again in 1910 with the Johnson-Jeffries heavyweight title bout.

But for Dempsey-Carpentier, Rickard saw a gold mine of humanity on the east coast. He settled on a site called Boyle's Thirty Acres, a lowland marsh area in Jersey City, New Jersey located just minutes from the population center of New York City.

He brought in the same crew he had used in Toledo for the Dempsey-Willard fight – the same crew that had built the Reno stadium for Johnson-Jeffries – to construct a 50,000-seat arena, but soon ordered it expanded to 90,000 seats when ticket sales boomed. The total cost for arena construction was $250,000. Fight tickets were $50 for ringside and scaled back from there to $40, $30, $20 and $15 for reserved seats. General admission seats were $5.50. Adjusted for inflation, that would be about $80 today. Ticket sales were so good that counterfeiting became a concern and Rickard had to place a notice in area newspapers warning of counterfeit tickets being sold.

The fight did draw opposition from "the morals crowd." William Crafts, who headed the International Reform Bureau in Washington, D.C., vowed to file court papers to block the fight and criminally indict all the principals involved, because such a match was nothing short of a dual assault.

As it turned out, Pierre Garvin, the Hudson County District Attorney, refused to prosecute the case and the fight went on.

Garvin later became a divorce lawyer in Reno and told the story of the Dempsey-Carpentier fight to his fellow Kiwanis Club members in April 1931. "I saw no reason to try to stop the fight and believe my judgment was correct," he said. "In fact, I enjoyed the fight myself."

Even as the legal wrangling was going on, both fighters went into training. Kearns initially set up Dempsey's camp in Summit, New Jersey but soon moved it to Atlantic City, where spectators paid as much as a dollar to watch the champion train. Deschamps set up Carpentier's camp in nearby Manhasset and closed it to the public and the press. The rumor was that Carpentier was working on a secret punch that would knock out Dempsey.

Whether it was Rickard's promotion of the fight as good versus evil, the war hero versus the slacker or something else, the fight became the biggest story in the world. Newspapers from America to Europe to Japan carried daily stories and some in Europe complained the fight was getting more attention than the Treaty of Versailles. In Paris on the day of the fight, July 2, six military airplanes were on standby to announce the results, flashing red lights if their countryman was the winner or white lights if Dempsey was victorious.

The fight attracted everyone from high society to gangsters to Hollywood and vaudeville. Rickard personally escorted John D. Rockefeller to a premium seat. Roosevelts, Vanderbilts and Astors were joined by automobile giant Henry Ford and other blue bloods of the day. Tom Mix (who performed tricks with a Mexican hat between the preliminary bouts), Al Jolson, Owen Moore and George M. Cohan led the entertainment contingent. Government officials from Spain, Peru, Russia, the Netherlands and other countries were in attendance as well.

Tex Rickard was a nervous wreck. What if the arena collapsed from the sheer weight of the crowd? What if bad weather set in? And perhaps his greatest fear, what if Dempsey ended up killing Carpentier in the ring? He went to Dempsey's dressing room and pleaded with him to be careful. A preoccupied Dempsey ignored him. He would fight as he always did.

Rickard might have been overly cautious, but many in the press and the stands, were probably overly optimistic about Carpentier's chances. He was, after all, a light heavyweight and Dempsey outweighed him by 20 to 25 pounds. That physical difference was striking when the two fighters entered the right about 3 p.m. Their styles were also strikingly opposite once the gong clanged to open the bout. Carpentier was upright, his knees bent slightly to allow him to spring forward or back and follow his left jab with a hard right. Dempsey, meanwhile, was in his distinctive bob-and-weave pattern, looking to land either hand with maximum power.

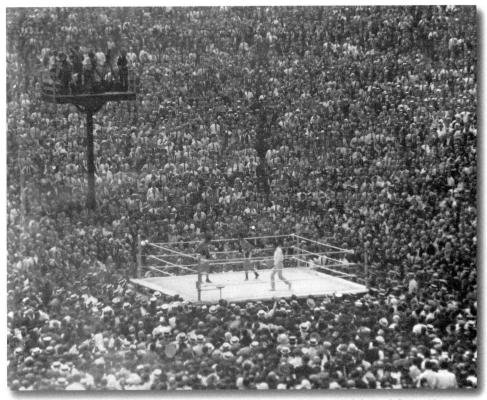

A massive crowd packs Boyles Thirty Acres for the Dempsey-Carpentier fight on July 2, 1921.
Colleen Rosencrantz Collection

In the first round, Carpentier used his springing style to land several punches to Dempsey's head. Dempsey, meanwhile concentrated on the body. When he did go to the head, he opened a cut over the Frenchman's right eye and bloodied his nose.

Dempsey stepped up his aggressiveness in the second round, but Carpentier was able to dance away from most of the rushes. Growing confident, Carpentier then went on the offensive and landed several combinations to Dempsey's head. He then threw his best punch of the fight, an overhand right to Dempsey's jaw. It hurt Dempsey slightly, but hurt Carpentier even more. He broke his thumb in two places and sprained his wrist. He could not follow up in any manner to take advantage of Dempsey's momentary weakness. Dempsey shook his head after the blow and continued forward. By the end of the round, Dempsey opened another cut on Carpentier's face.

In the third round, Dempsey was in complete control, ripping both hands to the challenger's body. It ended in the fourth. The champion floored Carpentier with a right to the jaw. The challenger sprang to his feet at the count of nine, but Dempsey continued his unrelenting assault to the body and floored Carpentier with another right to the jaw. This time, the challenger could not get up. The Battle of the Century was over and Jack Dempsey, hero or villain, was the undisputed champion.

The fight's gate was $1,895,733 – the first million-dollar gate in the history of boxing – more than twice the $800,000 offered by the speculators in Broken Hills.

Still, the Nevada speculators might have considered themselves lucky in hindsight two years later. The oil-rich town of Shelby, Montana lured Dempsey for a title defense against Tommy Gibbons on July 4, 1923, and suffered a financial disaster from the fight.

Doc Kearns, convinced he would handle the bout without any help from Tex Rickard, held fast to a $250,000 demand for Dempsey's share. They were paid $200,000 in advance and agreed, reluctantly by Kearns, to take the rest out of the gate receipts.

Dempsey won the fight by way of a 15-round decision, but the fight was a financial calamity for Shelby and nearby Great Falls – and for Gibbons, who was paid nothing. Four banks went belly-up, all of them blaming financing of the fight for their failure.

Shelby recovered financially from the disaster over the next several years. That could not be said for Broken Hills. The mines, never very lucrative from the start, eventually played out and, like many other Nevada boomtowns, Broken Hills faded into history. Today, it is marked only by a few building foundations, an abandoned graveyard and mention in books on Nevada ghost towns.

The fight game, propelled by Jack Dempsey and Tex Rickard, was moving east.

9

A Manager Lost, A Wife Gained

After the debacle in Shelby, Montana, Dempsey was eager to put the promotion of his battles back in the hands of Tex Rickard. In fact, Dempsey's unconditional confidence in Doc Kearns as his manager was starting to show cracks. Since they initially hooked up in 1917, the pair had split Dempsey's earnings 50-50, an unusually high percentage for a manager. In addition, Kearns had always taken "expenses" out of Dempsey's share of the earnings. Many people, Rickard among the most vocal, started telling Dempsey that Kearns was robbing him blind. After Shelby, Dempsey was starting to listen.

On July 12, 1923, just a few days after the Dempsey-Gibbons bout, former heavyweight champion Jess Willard attempted a comeback at Boyle's Thirty Acres in Jersey City, the same site as the Dempsey-Carpentier fight. In a fight promoted by Rickard – and attended by a massive crowd of 80,000 – Willard was matched against a relatively unknown South American boxer named Luis Angel Firpo. In the eighth round, a wild right from Firpo – whose buzzsaw style earned him the nickname the Wild Bull of the Pampas – landed squarely on Willard's jaw. The former champion went down and was unable to get back up before being counted out. The massive crowd cheered the fearless young victor.

It was the final fight of Willard's career, save for one exhibition bout a few years later, but it was just the beginning for Firpo. Both Rickard and Kearns, who had been ringside for the bout, saw the Argentine as the perfect opponent for Dempsey's next title defense, and the sooner the better. Within

Jack Dempsey and his wife, Estelle Taylor, starred together in the film "Manhattan Madness."
Colleen Rosencrantz Collection

days, the fight was set for September 14 at the Polo Grounds in New York City. Dempsey was guaranteed $500,000 for the fight and Firpo guaranteed $200,000.

Though the maximum ticket price allowed by New York law was $27.50, advanced ticket sales for the fight reached more than $1 million, much to the delight of Rickard. Ticket speculators were getting more than $200 for ringside seats.

More than 88,000 spectators packed into the stadium and they weren't disappointed. The fight, though it didn't last two full rounds, is still talked about with reverence more than 80 years later for its sheer ferocity and for solidifying Dempsey's legend in the ring.

As soon as the bell sounded to start the fight, Dempsey rushed across the ring and threw a looping right at the challenger's head. Firpo side-stepped it and answered with a left uppercut that landed squarely on Dempsey's jaw. The fight was 10 seconds old and Dempsey was on the canvas. Eighty-eight thousand spectators all stood in amazement and didn't sit down for the remainder of the fight. Dempsey was up before the referee could start his count and was back on the attack in a rage. Within seconds, a right hook sent Firpo down for a count of nine. The fight was about 40 seconds old. Another series of combinations sent Firpo down again and again he got up. The fighters went into a clinch and when referee Johnny Gallagher broke them, Firpo stepped back and dropped his hands. It was a bad mistake as Dempsey whipped an uppercut to his chin and Firpo hit the deck for a third time.

The rules of boxing at this time still did not require a boxer to go to a neutral corner. Usually, the fighter who scored the knockdown hovered over his opponent to sock him again as soon as the opponent stood up. Dempsey liked to circle behind his opponents – as he had done so effectively in the Willard fight. As Firpo rose, Dempsey knocked him down again, and then again with a vicious uppercut Firpo never saw coming. But Firpo was game and this time when he got up, he came up swinging and caught Dempsey with a right, knocking him to his knees. Again Dempsey sprang up and landed a hard body shot. Firpo ignored it and threw a series of clubbing rights that forced Dempsey against the ropes. Then another right hand, more a push than a punch, sent the off-balance Dempsey between the top and middle ropes and completely out of the ring.

"I went out of the ring backward, between the top and middle ropes, and landed on my neck on (*New York Tribune* reporter) Jack Lawrence's typewriter in the first row of the press section," Dempsey recalled in his autobiography. "I don't remember getting back into the ring."

With a push from Lawrence and a Western Union operator sitting next to Lawrence, Dempsey was back in the ring at the count of nine, though he said he didn't remember anything from the time he was sent out of the ring until he was sitting on his stool in the corner between the first and second rounds. He had to ask Jack Kearns and Joe Benjamin, who were arguing over the location of the smelling salts, what round it was.

The second round started the way the first had ended, with both fighters throwing haymakers and disregarding any defense whatsoever. They clinched twice, the second time, Dempsey literally throwing Firpo to the canvas. Firpo rose and rushed in, only to be caught with a Dempsey left that sent him falling toward the canvas. Before he hit, Dempsey added a right hook. At the count of ten, Firpo was still struggling to get up and the crowd roared as Dempsey was declared the winner.

Sportswriters called the first round the greatest in the history of the sport. It later sparked rule changes, including a fighter being required to go to a neutral corner when the opponent is knocked down instead of standing over him as Dempsey had done.

Dempsey wasn't worried about the rules. He was worried about the purse, however. Prior to the fight, he told Rickard that he, not Kearns, would be collecting the purse from the fight. Rickard, who didn't much care for Kearns anyway, happily agreed. Kearns was outraged the next day when Rickard informed him he'd already given the money to Dempsey. Kearns went to Dempsey, who gave the manager his split, but there were angry words exchanged.

"I wasn't going to get excited," Dempsey recalled in his autobiography. "I counted out what was coming to him and took what he owed me. This time I got more than he did and it burned him.

"'What the hell you going to do with that money?' he yelled at me.

"'Well, I'm putting two hundred thousand in a trust fund,' I said.

"'What interest?

"'I dunno. Three-four-five percent, whatever I'm going to get.'

"Doc looked at me like I was dirt.

"'You damn fool,' he said, shaking his head. 'I could get you fifteen percent.'

"I had to say it then or maybe never.

"'Doc,' I said. 'I'm going to put that money where I know I'll have it when I'm old.'

"He blew. Hot as hell."

After the Firpo fight, Dempsey was, without question, the most famous athlete in the country – more famous than Babe Ruth (who was at the fight), Bill Tilden, Bobby Jones, Red Grange or any of the stars of the day. He'd just made $500,000 and was ready to enjoy his riches. That quest eventually led him away from New York and back to the West Coast, with a stop in between to accept an invitation from President Calvin Coolidge to visit the White House.

Dempsey bought a large home on Western Avenue in Los Angeles and moved his mother, sister, and several of his brothers there with him. The biggest Hollywood stars of the day – Douglas Fairbanks, Tom Mix, Charlie

Chaplain and Mary Pickford – were his friends. Dozens of old pugs and sports writers became constant figures at his home, where he maintained a steady supply of food and booze for everyone, telling his mother, "a champion needs to live like a champion."

Celia Dempsey, a strict Mormon who was in her 70s by then, put up with the situation for about a year before returning to Utah where Dempsey bought her a 22-acre farm outside Salt Lake City.

In the meantime, he had signed a $1 million contract with Carl Laemmle, the president of Universal Studios, to make 10 films – an incredible sum for 1924. He was linked romantically to numerous starlets, but one, in particular, became the focus of his affections. Estelle Taylor was a dark-haired beauty with a quick wit and burning ambition that surpassed her talents as an actress. Dempsey fell for her head over heels.

Doc Kearns was far less enamored with Estelle and the feeling was mutual. Kearns was enraged when Dempsey informed him of their engagement and went so far as to hire a private detective to look into Estelle's background. Estelle didn't trust Kearns and felt he epitomized everything she hated about boxing.

The two had a public blowup at the Montmartre Club on Hollywood Boulevard with Dempsey caught in the middle. A drunken, belligerent Kearns insulted Estelle and her plans for she and Dempsey to make a movie together. Estelle stormed from the club, Dempsey with her, and issued him an ultimatum when they arrived back at her apartment: it was her or Kearns. Dempsey ultimately sided with Estelle and his long partnership with Kearns came to an abrupt end.

Kearns wasn't about to go quietly, however. He slapped Dempsey with lawsuit upon lawsuit, vowing that Dempsey was a bum when he found him and would be again without him. Dempsey and Estelle were married on Feb. 7, 1925 in San Diego, a few weeks after his split with Kearns.

It was a tumultuous marriage from the start – a marriage that would eventually lead Jack Dempsey back to Nevada.

Challenger Jack Dempsey stands above heavyweight champion Gene Tunney during the famous "long-count" fight in Chicago in 1927. *Reno Gazette-Journal File*

10
'Honey, I Forgot to Duck'

If the whole country was watching Jack Dempsey's actions in Hollywood – and wondering when he'd be getting back into the ring – one person in particular was studying his every move, but not in Hollywood. Gene Tunney, the former light-heavyweight champion had his eyes on Dempsey's title. In fact, he had coveted it for years. Nicknamed "The Fighting Marine," Tunney fought on the undercard of Dempsey-Carpentier fight and had attended the Dempsey-Firpo fight to closely study the champion. Far ahead of his time, Tunney studied the films of Dempsey's bouts, taking note of the champion's mannerisms and tendencies that might allow a challenger an advantage.

What's more, Tunney had Tex Rickard in his corner and Rickard had a strong desire to make the match. There were problems, however. The press was demanding a fight between Dempsey and Harry Wills, who they had dubbed the top contender. Wills was black and Rickard, still gun-shy from the race riots that followed the Johnson-Jeffries fight in Reno in 1910, vowed he would never promote such a bout. The New York State Athletic Commission stripped the idle Dempsey of his boxing license, prohibiting Rickard from holding a Dempsey-Tunney fight anywhere in the state. So Rickard went looking elsewhere and found a home for the bout in Philadelphia, which was celebrating its sesquicentennial in 1926.

In addition to his split with Kearns, Dempsey was also without a trainer. Teddy Hayes, who had been with Dempsey since he won the title and also managed Dempsey's business in Hollywood, did not want Dempsey to get into the ring with Tunney, a skilled boxer, without a tuneup bout or two. When Dempsey ignored Hayes' requests, Hayes split with the champion.

Dempsey was confident there were no legitimate challengers out there for him and felt he could lick any fighter Rickard sent into the ring to face him.

Jim Coffroth, at one time the biggest boxing promoter in the country before Rickard claimed the title, took an interest in Dempsey and offered the services of Gene Normile to be Dempsey's manager. Coffroth had retired from the boxing promotion business and was running a successful horse racing track across the Mexican border from San Diego called Agua Caliente.

There was one significant problem with Normile: he was not a boxing man. Jack Kearns, despite all his bluster, knew the fight game and would have insisted Dempsey take one or more warm-up bouts before taking on Tunney. Without Kearns, Dempsey was making all the boxing decisions and felt all he had to do was get his body in shape and he would be ready for Tunney. He didn't feel ring rust would be a problem at all and admitted years later it was a big mistake.

The fight was set for September 23, 1926 at the newly constructed Sesquicentennial Stadium in Philadelphia. Fans were eager – indeed impatient – to see Dempsey back in the ring. The champion had been inactive for three years and there were calls for him to give up his title if he wasn't going to defend it.

Despite the inactivity and despite the lack of any sort of tune-up fight, Dempsey was made an overwhelming favorite to retain his title. On the day of the fight, which dawned dark and rainy, Dempsey was listed as a 4-to-1 favorite. Sportswriters and bettors believed that despite his layoff, Dempsey's now-legendary punching power would make the difference. The Associated Press summed it up this way the day before the fight when the odds were 3-to-1:

> … Invariably the fight enthusiast comes back to the belief that Dempsey's punch, the sock that put Jess Willard, Georges Carpentier and Luis Firpo on the floor a dozen or more times, will end the battle of the sesqi.
>
> Among newspaper critics, among the men who have been backing their opinions in wagers at odds of as high and three to one on the champion and among the "wise men" of the boxing game, there is almost universal conviction that Dempsey will win by a knockout inside of four rounds.

The prognosticators couldn't have been more wrong. During Dempsey's layoff, Tunney had fought 17 times, including two memorable battles with Harry Greb, the Pittsburgh Windmill, and a 15-round knockout victory over Georges Carpentier. Tunney entered the fight with a quiet confidence.

Dempsey, meanwhile, was under stress from numerous distractions. Without a boxing man as his manager, he was making all the decisions himself. In addition, Doc Kearns was making trouble, filing multiple lawsuits to try to have the fight stopped. Dempsey was having intestinal problems from the stress and drinking olive oil to settle his stomach. On fight day, shortly after his morning shot of olive oil, he began to suffer from cramps. Speculation persists to present day that a bodyguard, Mike Trent, was paid off to put something into the olive oil. Dempsey always said it wouldn't have mattered.

The largest crowd in boxing history – officially listed at 120,757, but considered as large as 135,000 because of gate-crashers, newspapermen, policemen, ushers and other non-paying witnesses – turned out for the late-night battle that was scheduled to begin at 9 p.m. Even the great showman Rickard gasped at the size of the crowd, which included the elite of society from politics to industry to sports to entertainment. Babe Ruth was there as were William Randolph Hearst, Tom Mix and Charlie Chaplin to name a few. The purse was a record $1,895,733.

At least one Nevada resident was at the fight. John T. McDuff of Reno wired friends immediately after the fight and said, "it was a great battle and Tunney's fight all the way." A month later, McDuff was visiting family in Rhode Island and suffered a broken arm. The *Reno Evening Gazette* identified him as "the only Reno resident to attend the Dempsey-Tunney fight in Philadelphia."

Millions of Americans listened to the radio broadcast. In Northern Nevada, hundreds of fans crowded in front of Reno's two newspapers to hear announcers bellow round-by-round reports of the fight ripped from dispatches from The Associated Press. Both the *Reno Evening Gazette* and *Nevada State Journal* – bitter enemies – had their presses prepared to print "extras" as soon as the fight ended.

It was drizzling rain in Philadelphia as the fighters entered the ring. Tunney, wearing a robe with a Marines insignia on the back was given a huge ovation as he made the long walk from his dressing room. Dempsey received a colder reception, including many boos when he made his way to the ring. The two fighters met in the middle of the ring. "Hello champion," Tunney said. "Hello Gene," Dempsey replied.

The first round set the tone for the rest of the fight. About a minute in, Tunney caught Dempsey with a lead right that landed on Dempsey's cheekbone and buckled his knees. Both fighters said later that if it had landed on his chin, Dempsey would have been knocked out. Tunney's confidence grew from there, and Dempsey, slowed by sickness and a lack of ring activity could never get untracked against his quicker opponent.

Dempsey said he could never get comfortable footing in the wet ring. By the middle rounds of the 10-round bout, the drizzle had escalated to a downpour, but it didn't seem to bother Tunney, who Dempsey described as skating around the ring like a champion ice skater. Ever the aggressor, Dempsey tried to bore in, but Tunney danced away and scored easily with jabs and combinations. By the late rounds, every rush from the beaten and battered Dempsey was met with a flurry of punches from Tunney.

At the final bell, Dempsey put his arm around Tunney and said, "Good fight, Gene. You won." In fact, Tunney had won all 10 rounds on the judges' scorecards.

Talking to reporters afterward, Dempsey was candid. "It's the old story. The best man won," Dempsey said. "I have no alibis. Give all the credit to Gene. He's a great champion."

Both Reno newspapers had extras on the streets within minutes and both bragged that the fans outside their respective establishments had been with Tunney from the start.

Estelle Taylor did not attend the fight and learned of her husband's defeat at the train station in Fort Wayne, Indiana, where she was in transit to Philadelphia. When she finally arrived at the hotel the next day, she called her husband by the pet name she had for him and asked, "What happened, Ginsberg?" Dempsey replied with a most memorable line. "Honey, I forgot to duck." (Years later, President Ronald Reagan borrowed the line after he was shot by would-be assassin John Hinkley.)

It was how he handled the defeat as much as anything that endeared Dempsey to many fight fans. During his reign as champion, he was often booed and could hear the "slacker" catcalls from the streets and the crowds at his matches. But he said there was a marked change as he was exiting the ring as the dethroned champion. "Something happened that had never happened to me before," he wrote in his 1959 autobiography. "The people were cheering for me, clapping for me, calling out my name in a way I had never heard before. I never realized how much I had hungered for a sound like that, and now here it was – on the night I blew my title. Losing was the making of me."

It wasn't long before calls started for a rematch. Rickard, however, was cautious. Dempsey had lost and lost badly and was giving honest consideration to quitting. He had returned to Los Angeles. He trained little, mostly with road work to keep his weight down. Some reporters referred to him as "the hollow shell of Hollywood."

Rickard reasoned that an immediate rematch with Tunney might not draw much public appeal. Instead, the old promoter devised an "elimination tournament." Originally, Rickard's plans included Basque heavyweight Paulino Uzcudun, but eventually, Rickard decided the first elimination match would feature young contender Jack Sharkey, the Boston Gob, and Jim Maloney in a bout in May 1927. The winner of that fight would face Dempsey in late July and the victor would then be matched with Tunney in September for the title.

In the meantime, Dempsey's physical wounds and his pride had healed. He hired a new manager in Leo P. Flynn and a new trainer in Gus Wilson to get him into boxing shape.

Sharkey knocked out Maloney in the fifth round and Rickard scheduled a Sharkey-Dempsey bout for July 21 at Yankee Stadium in New York. What Rickard realized in the interim is that Dempsey's popularity had not waned since he lost the title. Ticket sales were brisk and ticket brokers were selling the $27.50 ringside seats for $200 as fight day approached.

Dempsey went into serious training at Saratoga Lake, dutifully following a strict regimen set up by Flynn. He worked himself into good shape and was in good spirits, but just three weeks before the fight, a family tragedy shook Dempsey to the core. His brother Johnny, staying just 20 miles from Dempsey's training camp, murdered his wife and then turned the gun on himself, the end result of a life ruined by heroin addiction. Dempsey had to identify the bodies and make the call to his mother with the news. He also had to make arrangements to ship Johnny's body back to Salt Lake for burial.

Dempsey was devastated and went into seclusion at his camp for two days. On the Fourth of July, he resumed training, but closed his camp to the public. He wanted to train without distraction.

Bettors were clearly worried about Dempsey's physical and mental state as the fight loomed. The 28-year-old Sharkey was made anywhere from a $2-to-1 to a 7-to-5 favorite. Like Tunney, Sharkey entered the fight against Dempsey on a winning streak. He had won 13 consecutive fights and hadn't lost in two years. Three of those victories – including one over Harry Wills – the black fighter Dempsey was often accused of ducking – came as the result of a foul. In the Wills fight, held Oct. 12, 1926 in Brooklyn, Sharkey fell to the canvas clutching his groin in the 13th round and was awarded the victory, a controversial decision some ringside reporters said because they had seen no low blow.

Still, Sharkey was supremely confident heading into the fight with Dempsey, telling reporters he was going to knock Dempsey out and then move on to Tunney. The fight drew an estimated 82,000 people and a gate of $1,083,530 – the first-ever million-dollar gate for a non-title bout. As had become the norm for a Dempsey fight, the elite of the nation turned out, including future president Franklin D. Roosevelt. Reigning champion Gene Tunney was there to watch as well.

In the first round, Sharkey's prediction appeared it would come true. The Associated Press described it in its round-by-round dispatch:

> Dempsey came out in a crouch and fell into a clinch, hammering five short rights to the body as Sharkey missed a left hook.
>
> Dempsey bored in again, drilling hard smashes to the ribs. (Sharkey) hooked two lefts to Dempsey's head. They were close again and Sharkey got in two more to the head.
>
> Sharkey stabbed Dempsey with a left to the head. Dempsey bored in again, took two lefts to the head and again drove short punches to Sharkey's body. Sharkey looked tired. Sharkey licked Jack with two right uppercuts.
>
> Dempsey, reeling and groggy, moved about the ring under a fuselage. Sharkey smashed him again with rights. Dempsey was groggy as Sharkey missed a long right. The bell caught Sharkey halfway through a right swing. Dempsey returned to his corner very tired.

The first round set the tone for the next four as Sharkey pounded Dempsey to the head almost at will. Dempsey, already bleeding from the mouth after the first round, was cut under the right eye in the third. That cut was bleeding badly in the fourth.

Taking punishment was nothing new for Dempsey, who often took multiple blows as he worked to get inside against opponents. The difference between this bout and the Tunney bout is that Dempsey was able to score with his body blows against Sharkey and by the end of the fifth round, they were clearly starting to take a toll. However, the end of the sixth round was nearly the end of the fight as Sharkey landed a solid uppercut that snapped Dempsey's head back. Reporters described it as "the cleanest and hardest punch of the fight" up to that point.

In the seventh round, Dempsey again came out and forced the action, smashing punches to Sharkey's body and forcing Sharkey to get into a clinch. Suddenly, Dempsey whipped a right to the body – a punch that some observers said was clearly low while others said was clearly fair. When it landed, a pained Sharkey dropped his gloves and turned toward referee Jack O'Sullivan to complain. It was a critical mistake as Dempsey ripped a short left hook to Sharkey's jaw. Sharkey dropped as if he'd been shot and O'Sullivan counted him out.

Questioned later about whether he should have hit Sharkey when he dropped his gloves, Dempsey replied, "What was I supposed to do, write him a letter?" From his earliest fights in mining camps of Colorado and Nevada, Dempsey never gave favors in the ring and never expected any for himself. Reporters allowed to view the fight films the next day concluded no foul was committed.

One expert at ringside – champion Gene Tunney – concurred with the sportswriters. He said Dempsey's body shot was fair. Tunney was impressed with Dempsey's performance overall, particularly with the power in the decisive left hook. "Did you notice how far that last blow carried?" Tunney asked. "Not very far, not many inches, but oh what power there was behind it. Yes, Dempsey can hit. He always has been able to hit and I suppose he always will be as long as he stays in there."

"I've never seen him fight better," Tunney said, perhaps starting the buildup for their September rematch, which Tex Rickard scheduled for Chicago's Soldier Field on September 22, 1927. Rickard did not want to hold the fight in New York for two main reasons: the maximum $27.50 ticket price New York allowed and the fact that no venue in New York could hold the crowd Rickard was envisioning. Chicago and its year-old stadium was the ideal place with seats for an unprecedented 150,000 or more fans.

Ticket prices were set at $40 for ringside and declined to $5 for the back seats, which patrons learned on the night of the fight "offered a view of all except for the fight itself." By mid-September, Rickard was assured of the first $2 million gate in boxing history.

Enthusiasm for the fight was not an issue, but it was the challenger Dempsey, and not the champion Tunney, who was the source of that enthusiasm. While Tunney's victory in Philadelphia was cheered, the champion did little to warm up to fans or newspapermen after claiming the title. In fact, many considered him arrogant and aloof, a "Fancy Dan" who quoted Shakespeare. Dempsey was seen as the working man's champion, a brawler from out of the wild west who fought with savagery inside the ring, but who was jovial and a man of the people outside it.

Dempsey set up training camp at the racetrack at Lincoln Fields, while Tunney settled in at the Cedar Crest Country Club, 52 miles from downtown Chicago.

Despite his public perception problem, Tunney was greeted to a hero's welcome when he arrived in town by train on September 2, 1927. He was met at the LaSalle Street Station by several thousand Chicago residents and more lined the streets as Tunney made his way to City Hall to meet Mayor "Big Bill" Thompson. Chicago newspapers compared the event to Lindberg's reception after he returned from crossing the Atlantic Ocean.

The rematch came down to one simple question, which the *Reno Evening Gazette* ran as a headline on the front page on the day of the fight: "Can Jack Do It?" No former heavyweight champion had ever reclaimed the title after losing it and Dempsey was now 32 years old. Almost from the start, there were rumors that the fight was fixed. When Al Capone visited Dempsey's camp and it was revealed he had bet heavily on Dempsey to win, the rumors grew stronger.

Tunney, too, was linked to unsavory characters, and an open letter attributed to Dempsey, but most likely written by his manager, Leo Flynn, appeared in the *Chicago Herald-Examiner* and asked Tunney to explain his relationship with gamblers Boo Boo Hoff and Abe Attell. Tunney responded with a letter of his own, calling the allegations trash and adding a snipe at the end that said, "P.S. I might add that I wrote this letter myself."

Rumors of potential foul play on both sides were rampant and Dempsey, wary from his bad olive oil experience in Philadelphia, was careful what he ingested. Trainer Jerry "The Greek" Luvadis was assigned to taste all Dempsey's food and sip from his drinks. As *New York Herald Tribune* sports editor W.O. McGeehan described it, "As long as the Greek lived, Dempsey could eat."

Fight day dawned cold and gray and during the undercard bouts, there were sprinkles of rain. Unlike Philadelphia, however, rain would not dampen the main event. As had become typical at Dempsey fights, the elite of society, industry, politics and sports turned out. Rickard remarked to Hype Igoe of the *New York World*, "Kid, if the earth came up and the sky came down and wiped out my first ten rows, it would be the end of everything. Because I've got in those first ten rows all the world's wealth, all the world's brains and production talent. Just in them ten rows, kid."

Hundreds of newspapermen attended and direct wires were set up at ringside to relay up-to-the-second updates to newspaper sites across the country, including Reno, where both the *Reno Evening Gazette* and *Nevada State Journal* planned to have announcers standing by to relay details to people in the streets. A live radio broadcast was also planned and more than a million people were expected to listen to the live coverage.

This time, Dempsey entered the ring first, and was greeted with a crescendo of cheers. Tunney, again wearing his robe with the Marine Corps insignia, received a quieter reception, far different than their fight in Philadelphia. The two exchanged a friendly greeting in the ring.

A brief ceremony included the introduction of former champions including Jack Johnson and Jim Jeffries of Reno fame and Battling Nelson, who had lost to Joe Gans in Goldfield years before.

Dave Barry was introduced as the referee and he instructed both men of the new rule that required a fighter who scores a knockdown to retreat to a neutral corner for the duration of the count. He also warned that rabbit punches and kidney punches would not be allowed. Both Dempsey and Tunney acknowledged that they understood the instructions.

Once the bell sounded, the fight looked much the same as the first bout in Philadelphia. Dempsey, bobbing and weaving, pressed the action. Tunney used his jab and quickness to keep the challenger away. Through six rounds, Tunney was clearly ahead. In fact, he was even more confident than he had been in Philadelphia and started taking the fight to Dempsey. It was almost his undoing.

About a minute into the seventh round, the opportunity Dempsey had been awaiting for two years – and a moment that has been debated for more than 80 years since – finally arrived like a bolt of lightning. As Tunney flicked a left jab, Dempsey beat him to the punch with looping right that landed on the left side of Tunney's face, knocking him off balance. Dempsey followed the right with a perfectly timed left hook that sent Tunney reeling into the ropes near Dempsey's corner. As the champion started to fall, Dempsey hit him four more times before Tunney finally crumpled to the canvas "like a falling tree" according to a *New York Times* report. Referee Dave Barry started the count, but immediately noticed that Dempsey had not gone to a neutral corner as the new rule required. Barry stopped his count and yelled at Dempsey, who was standing in his own corner, to move. The referee finally grabbed Dempsey by the arm and pointed him to a corner on the opposite side of the ring. When Barry returned, the knockdown timekeeper, Paul Beeler, was shouting "five," but Barry started his count at "one." Tunney, knocked off his feet for the first time in his career, had his left arm on the second rope. When Barry's revised count hit nine, Tunney sprung to his feet. By most estimates, he was on the canvas for between 14 and 18 seconds.

Dempsey rushed across the ring, but Tunney either tied him up or eluded the rushes for the rest of the round. By the eighth round, Tunney had recovered and a sharp blow knocked Dempsey down. As Dempsey went to the canvas, Barry immediately yelled "one" to start the count, not waiting for Tunney to go to a neutral corner. Dempsey was on his feet by the count of two and continued his chase of Tunney. He could never catch him and after 10 rounds, Tunney retained his title with a unanimous decision.

Afterward, Dempsey said of the long count, "If Gene got the benefit of that break, that was one of the breaks of the game, that was all." His handlers weren't nearling as understanding. Leo P. Flynn, his manager, filed an appeal with the Illinois State Athletic Commission arguing that Tunney had been down for more than 10 seconds in the seventh. Board chairman John C. Righeimer said he would not accept the protest and said that Dempsey had brought the problem on himself by not going to a neutral corner as instructed.

Dempsey's acceptance of the outcome as one of the breaks only enhanced his popularity. To many people, he was the true champion who had been robbed of the title by a crooked referee. Dempsey said years later that, even if the charge wasn't true, he appreciated having the fans on his side.

One of the first-hand witnesses to the long-count fight, knockdown timekeeper Paul Beeler, eventually settled in Nevada after a long career as a railroad man. Beeler, who lived in Sparks, related his memories of the fight to Reno newsman Ty Cobb in a 1969 interview. Cobb asked him perhaps the most important question: Could Tunney, without the benefit of the extra seconds, have gotten up by the count of 10? "I am sure he could have," Beeler said. "I was so close to him, I could have reached through the ropes and touched him. He was watching me count and his eyes were clear. He picked up my count and said 'six' with me. I know it would have been tough on Tunney if he had arisen right then. But he was smart. He took advantage of the extra time."

Beeler served as a timekeeper at numerous fights in the 1920s and 1930s. While he may have witnessed Dempsey's most famous defeat, his opinion of the former champion never changed as he told Cobb more than 40 years later: "Jack Dempsey was the greatest of all heavyweights. He could hit, he was fast and he could take it."

On September 26, 1927, Tex Rickard was back in New York and dreaming big of a third Dempsey-Tunney bout. This fight had drawn an official paid attendance of 104,943. The gate was $2,658,660. Tunney's share was

$990,445 and Dempsey's was $450,000, the most ever paid to a challenger in a championship fight. Tunney handed Tex Rickard a personal check for $9,555 and Rickard handed him a check for $1 million.

But it was Dempsey and not Tunney that was at the root of Rickard's third matchup dream. "Dempsey is still the greatest drawing card in the ring and is far from 'through' if he wishes to continue fighting," Rickard said.

Dempsey did not wish to continue. As he explained years later, "what happened in my case was that Miss Taylor wanted me to quit and I figured I had enough money."

That fact, however, was soon to change.

The Nevada State Journal announced Dempsey's plan to "rest" in Reno in 1931 with a banner headline. *Reno Gazette-Journal File*

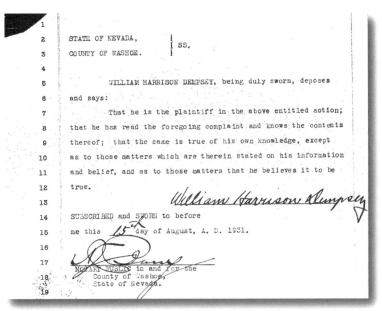

Jack Dempsey signed his given name, William Harrison Dempsey, on his divorce papers during his divorce from Estelle Taylor, 1931. *Author's Collection*

11
'A Six-Week Rest' in Reno

The late 1920s dealt Jack Dempsey a number of setbacks, and his two losses to Gene Tunney were comparatively minor among them. In 1928, at age 33 and a multi-millionaire, he announced his retirement from the ring, citing an eye problem that doctors said could lead to blindness if it was injured again. (Reno optometrist J. B. Gasho used Dempsey's eye problems to promote his business, running an advertisement in the Reno papers that included the pitch: "Due to defective eye muscles, Jack Dempsey is forced to give up boxing. Are your eyes forcing you out of the ring? Let us examine your eyes now.")

But Dempsey received a golden opportunity to stay involved in boxing. Tex Rickard, who had broken away from the Madison Square Garden Corporation after Gene Tunney's title defense against Tom Heeney on July 26, 1928 at Yankee Stadium was a financial failure, asked Dempsey to become his partner.

"I was as proud of that as anything in my life," Dempsey wrote in his 1959 autobiography. "When I was a bum being trucked through Goldfield in a wheelbarrow after my fight with Johnny Sudenberg, Tex had been far beyond me, the promoter of fights so big I could hardly understand them. Now there was his big hand shaking mine, and he was telling me I was his fifty-fifty partner until death. We never had a contract. You didn't need one with Tex Rickard."

One of their first promotions was to be the Jack Sharkey-Young Stribling fight in Miami in January of 1929, but Rickard didn't live to see it. He died on January 6, 1929 of peritonitis. "I wept like a kid," Dempsey said.

Dempsey carried on as a promoter and also had a number of other investments, including becoming a partner in Nevada mining ventures with George Wingfield, James McKay and William Graham of Reno. He invested in a Mexican resort on the Baja peninsula and also became involved in gambling at the Agua Caliente casino in Mexico. Wingfield, McKay, Graham and others in Reno also had interests in Agua Caliente, as did Gene Normile, Dempsey's manager during the Tunney fights and the right-hand man to race track man Jim Coffroth. Coffroth, who was originally from San Francisco, had been the top fight promoter in the country before Tex Rickard came along.

In May of 1929, word began to spread that Dempsey was considering a return to the ring and that Agua Caliente would be the site of the bout. The source of those rumors, Gene Normile, stopped in Reno on May 18, and a front-page story appeared in the *Nevada State Journal* the next day with the headline "Dempsey to Fight Again, Normile Asserts in Reno."

> Jack Dempsey, dethroned king of heavyweight battlers, will enter the ring again at Agua Caliente, Tia Juana's neighboring rival in Mexico, in an attempt to regain world's championship honors, according to an announcement made in Reno yesterday morning by Gene Normile, who was Dempsey's manager for the first Tunney fight.
>
> While in Reno, Normile showed friends an agreement signed by Dempsey which carries a million dollar guarantee for the former heavyweight king to meet an opponent at Agua Caliente at a time to be fixed later. Normile is reported to have said that the contract is a result of negotiations that started when the former champion was offered $800,000 to enter the ring at Agua Caliente and that the one million dollar figure was finally agreed upon.
>
> It is understood that those backing the proposed fight include Wirt G. Bowman, head of the syndicate which is promoting Agua Caliente, and Baron Long, race track man and owner of the U.S. Grant Hotel in San Diego. Bowman is related by marriage to Governor Rodriquez of Lower California.

Dempsey was in New York at the time of Normile's claims, but the former champion also made unpublicized trips to Reno that year "to check on my mining interests." On one visit, he was photographed by a young Gardnerville photographer named James A. Lawrence.

Whether the claims of Normile had any validity or not, such a fight never came off. Then, in October, the stock market crashed and changed everything.

By the turn of the year in 1930, Dempsey estimated he had lost $3 million with no end in sight. Though he still had the trust fund he had established after the Firpo fight, it was money he couldn't touch for years. "I was just like everyone else – broke," he said. He began refereeing boxing and wrestling matches across the country to make money. At the same time, his marriage to Estelle Taylor, which had been shaky for years, had unraveled to the point of no return, though in the press, both denied they were having any serious marital difficulties.

In the early months of 1931, Dempsey spent most of his time on the road. Though the appearances paled in comparison to the million-dollar gates during his title reign, Dempsey did make money off them. He was generally paid $5,000 and a percentage of the gate.

He maintained an interest in gambling and in March of 1931, that interest led him to Carson City, where the Nevada Legislature was considering a bill that would legalize gambling in the state. News reports appeared that Dempsey was considering either opening his own casino or joining with James McKay and Bill Graham as partners in one in Reno. The United Press put a story of his visit on the wires:

> RENO – Jack Dempsey may be considering establishing a high class gambling casino in Nevada if the "wide open" gambling bill is passed by the state legislature, it was rumored in Reno today (March 14).
>
> Dempsey arrived in Reno on Friday night and attended the boxing matches at the university. He held several "business conferences" with prominent gambling operators here and went to Carson City where he talked with legislators who are considering the bill.
>
> He left here today by airplane for Salt Lake City where he will visit with his mother. If he establishes a casino, Dempsey will be following the steps of his friend Tex Rickard, who once owned the Northern gambling

pavilion in the boom days of Goldfield in 1904, where 12 bartenders tended two 30-foot bars as housemen operated gambling tables.

Whether Dempsey, who met with legislators and Governor Fred Balzar, had any influence or not, the gambling bill passed a few days later and was signed into law by Balzar. The legislature also passed a bill that reduced the requirements to obtain a divorce in Nevada from three months to six weeks, the quickest time of any state in the union.

Dempsey had returned to the east, where his business manager, Leonard Sacks, had arranged a series of refereeing assignments for him. On April 7, 1931, Dempsey was in Columbus, Ohio to referee a bout between Bushy Graham and Johnny Farr, when he announced he was "going into absolute retirement from public life for at least two months on the order of his physicians at the Mayo Clinic in Rochester, Minn." Dempsey said he planned to "go to the country" to rest, but neither he nor Sacks would divulge the location. The answer came four days later with a banner headline on the front page of the *Nevada State Journal*: "Dempsey Due Today For Six Weeks Rest."

> SALT LAKE CITY, April 10–(AP)–Jack Dempsey, former world heavyweight champion, left tonight for Reno, Nevada, saying he intended to rest there for six weeks.
>
> He arrived from Chicago and spent eight hours at the home of his mother, Mrs. Celia Dempsey, before continuing his journey.
>
> Dempsey said he will resume refereeing of boxing and wrestling matches after his rest. He refused to discuss his matrimonial affairs.
>
> Dempsey was in Reno several weeks ago and at that time stated that he was just visiting former friends and attending to mining interests.

Upon his arrival in Reno, Dempsey again denied any marital troubles, telling the *Reno Evening Gazette*, "Estelle and I have had a scrap, but it was not a serious one, and there is always a chance of reconciliation. I came here with the idea of taking a rest and will spend much of my time fishing and hunting..."

That night, he was interviewed on KOH radio by Earl Leif, Nevada manager of United Press, and again denied he was in town for a divorce, insisting instead that he was in town on the advice of his doctors at the

Mayo Clinic. On the same radio program, Leonard Sacks insisted that Jack and Estelle were still very much in love.

People in Reno, meanwhile, were excited about the champion's visit. The *Nevada State Journal* reported: "Crowds of fans thronged the studio to hear and see the popular hero of the nation's sporting public and a spontaneous round of applause greeted him upon his appearance."

He had checked into the Riverside Hotel and spent his first day in "business meetings" with Bill Graham and others.

On April 14, he filed for divorce and announced he was leasing the Steinmiller home in Reno's mansion district on California Avenue. His rent was $1,000 per month, a princely sum for 1931.

The April 15 edition of the *Reno Evening Gazette* carried a story with the headline "Dempsey Selects Attorney and Then Goes Fishing." The attorney was Robert E. Burns of Reno, who the *Gazette* identified as an "old-time friend" of Dempsey's. Dempsey issued a brief statement to reporters. "I'm through talking and all information concerning this divorce business will be given out by Mr. Burns, who is my legal representative," he said.

If Dempsey thought he was going to slip into a quiet life in Reno to wait out his residency requirement for divorce, he was mistaken. His divorce plans made front-page news around the country and in particular in Reno and Los Angeles, where Estelle resided. Immediately there were rumors that another woman, a blonde, was the cause of the breakup. One of Burns' first acts was to deny the rumors. He told reporters that such rumors were "absurd." Still, photos of Elizabeth Church, a Pittsburgh divorcee, appeared in papers around the country with captions linking her to Dempsey in Reno.

Dempsey, who had always enjoyed the night life of New York and Los Angeles, found plenty of opportunity in Reno. With the new divorce laws, the town was literally teeming with women, and Jack Dempsey was rich, handsome and worldly. One of his favorite night spots was the New York Club, at 224 North Center Street, which opened soon after his arrival. The club catered to women, both sophisticated local women and those in town "for the cure." Many movie stars frequented the club when they were in town, and Dempsey still had plenty of friends in Hollywood.

Dempsey said years later that he wasn't dating one woman when he moved to Reno. He was dating numerous women. "Rather than stay in a hotel, I rented a house in Reno," he wrote in his 1977 autobiography. "I started taking out various women, whereupon the press predicted that each one would shortly become my fiancé. This didn't do my divorce plans or my privacy any good."

Dempsey was 35 and long removed from the days when he ate his first Reno meal in a hobo jungle. He was twice-married and soon to be twice-divorced. He'd traveled the world, given thousands of interviews, fought in front of the largest crowds in the history of boxing, and made and lost millions of dollars. Yet at his core, Dempsey was still a man of the west and he fit like a glove into Reno. He loved the outdoors and took advantage of the fishing and hunting opportunities. One of his frequent companions on such trips was Governor Fred Balzar. A photo of the two in a playful fighting pose at Pyramid Lake is included in Balzar's profile in a book on Nevada's governors.

The Reno newspapers and wire services took photos of him fishing the Truckee River and mowing the lawn at the home he was renting on California Avenue in Reno's mansion district. Universal Services motion picture editor Louella Parsons visited Reno and her story, which appeared in papers on the coast said, "Jack Dempsey is followed all over town by reporters, by women who are there to get divorced from their husbands, and others with some scheme to promote. Mr. Dempsey doesn't look to the right or left and seems annoyed at the attention of these busy females."

Dempsey was in demand from the local service clubs to be a speaker at their events and Reno's socialites enjoyed having him in their company. Dempsey, who truly enjoyed socializing with people from all classes, accommodated as many requests as he could, some more unusual than others.

"I had Jack Dempsey for a babysitter once," recalled Reno's Bill Griswold, whose father, Morley Griswold, was the state's lieutenant governor in 1931. "He was going out on the town with my parents and another couple. My parents had to go and pick up the real babysitter and Jack Dempsey sat there with my sister and me until our parents got back."

Dempsey spoke to students at the University of Nevada after receiving an invitation from student body president Ed Cantlon, who recalled his nervous first encounter with the former champion in his oral history years later.

> I called him about two o'clock (in the) afternoon and found him to be a most gracious and cooperative gentleman. He invited me to come up to his room and to talk to him in person rather than talk to him over the telephone. I had a delightful session with him, and he agreed to come to the next student body meeting.
>
> He said, "I'm no great public speaker, but I'm interested in the student activities. Instead of trying to

write a speech, why don't I just come and talk off-hand and give you kind of a pep talk about athletics and student affairs in general."

One of the things that he asked was, "Well, what time do you have this meeting?"

I said, "Oh, the meeting will be at 11:30 on a Thursday morning."

"Well that's fine," he said, "I won't have to shave twice. If your meeting was going to be in the afternoon, you'd have to give me a little leeway because I'd have to shave before coming." He had a very thick, black growth of whiskers.

He talked for about twelve to fifteen minutes and the student body meeting room was packed to overflowing that day, which it seldom was. Although I can't think of anything momentous that he said that day, it was a great stimulus for all of the students and was a great talking point for the rest of the year. I have a picture of his appearance on the front steps of the education building. He only went about to the fourth or fifth grade in school, and I don't know what Katie Riegelhuth would have thought about his grammar and diction, but he talked quite fluently and was quite articulate.

Even a minor traffic accident was cause for Reno citizens to celebrate their newfound favorite son. The *Reno Evening Gazette* reported it this way:

The large slate-colored car owned by James McKay and operated jointly by McKay and Jack Dempsey came to grief late yesterday afternoon at the corner of Virginia and Stewart Streets and gave a crowd a thrill when Dempsey climbed out of the machine to survey the damage.

The big machine, headed north on Virginia Street, and a small car driven by George Luke of Fallon, came together unexpectedly. No one was hurt but the impact crumpled a front fender on each machine. Traffic was blocked by the crowd that quickly gathered as Luke was told by McKay and Dempsey to take his car to the nearest mechanic to get it repaired.

On April 23, 1931, Dempsey spoke to the Reno Kiwanis Club at the request of entertainment chairman Howard S. Doyle. The overflowing crowd enjoyed his stories of his early boxing adventures in Nevada, but it was his revelation about the Reno of 1931 that excited them the most.

"I like the climate here and have a high regard for the state of Nevada and her people," Dempsey said. "I have decided to buy myself a home here and it is going to be on the Nevada side." He said essentially the same thing when he addressed the Reno Rotary Club a few days later.

Several family members – including his brother, Bernie, sister, Elsie, and nephew, Lloyd Stannard, eventually joined him in town. Jack, Elsie and Lloyd hosted a reunion of former Colorado residents at Bowers Mansion.

Another thing that attracted Dempsey to Reno was the fact that, unlike other areas of the country that were feeling the effects of the Great Depression, Reno was bustling with the divorce trade and legalized gambling business. That meant there was money to be made and if his long associations with Tex Rickard and Jack Kearns taught him anything, it was how to make money. Dempsey, with partners Jim McKay, Bill Graham, George Wingfield, Nick Abelman and others, put together a plan to do just that. For the first time since the Johnson-Jeffries fight of 1910, Reno was about to return to the spotlight of the boxing world.

12
Jack the Promoter

Jack Dempsey had been in Reno all of three days when a rumor started circulating that plans were being considered for a heavyweight fight in Reno sometime during the summer. It was not idle chit-chat as one of the people prompting the rumor was James McKay. On April 15, 1931, a small article appeared in the Reno Evening Gazette under the headline "Plans considered for heavyweight fight here."

> Acting on the suggestion of Jack Dempsey, a group of Reno sportsmen including James McKay, William Graham and others are discussing the possibilities of holding a championship heavyweight prize fight here this summer with Dempsey as the referee.
>
> The plans are still very indefinite, McKay said today, and possibly there is not time enough before July 4 to prepare for the contest.
>
> Primo Carnera and George Godfrey are being considered as the possible contenders, although neither one of them have been advised so far.
>
> Whether Dempsey will act as promoter of the fight, if it is decided to hold one, or a company organized to handle the financial arrangements of the affair has not been considered.

> In fact, the proposal is so indefinite now that noth-
> ing may be done, but it is being seriously considered,
> McKay said.

Behind the scenes, plans were well under way. The term "sportsman" was used by newspapers as a polite way to describe gamblers and in 1931 Reno, Graham and McKay were at the forefront of gambling in Reno. (They had been at the forefront even before gambling was legalized by the 1931 Legislature, but the passage of the gambling bill gave them legitimacy.) They owned the Bank Club, 239 N. Center Street, the city's largest casino, and several speak-easies, including the Willows nightclub, which became a popular hangout for the divorce crowd. They also controlled the prostitution racket in Reno, including 50 cribs in a compound known as "The Stockade." They also were said to control the import of liquor into Reno and had a long-running and well-publicized battle with U.S. Attorney George Springmeyer.

They were said to be partners, or at least associates, of George Wingfield, who controlled the banks in Reno and was widely considered the political boss of the state. For a time, the heads of both the Democratic and Republican parties had offices in the same building as Wingfield and used the same phone number. Other silent partners of Graham and McKay included Tex Hall, who ran the prostitution business for the pair, and Nick Abelman, a savvy casino owner who had been in Goldfield and Tonopah during their heydays before relocating to Reno.

Historians have varying takes on Graham and McKay's place in Reno history. Some have called them mobsters and others simply refer to them as businessmen. In 1934, they were put on trial and, after two mistrials and five years, convicted of mail fraud and sent to prison. During their first trial, a key witness, banker Roy Frisch, disappeared under mysterious circumstances, never to be heard from again. (Although family members still leave a light on 75 years later.)

Dempsey, who was called as a defense witness during all three trials, often referred to the group in his later years as "The Syndicate." Though he maintained friendships with all the men for the rest of their lives and visited them whenever he was in Reno, he never mentioned any of them in his autobiographies.

On May 1, 1931, the rumors of a Fourth of July prizefight in Reno became a reality. The *Reno Evening Gazette* carried the story on page 16 of that day's edition.

> Definite announcement was made this morning by
> Jack Dempsey that a heavyweight boxing contest would

be held at the Reno Race Track on July 4 between two outstanding contenders in the heavyweight field.

Leonard Sacks, Dempsey's manager, will be manager in charge of the affair and James McKay and William Graham will be associated with Dempsey in promoting the fight. The contest will be from twenty to twenty-five rounds. Sacks said efforts are being made now to secure outstanding fighters for the main event.

Jack Dempsey points from the Reno Race Track and Bill Graham, left, and James McKay look on. *Colleen Rosencrantz Collection*

Among those being considered are Jack Sharkey, Jimmie Malone, Ernie Schaff, Paulino Uzcudun, Max Baer, Tommy Loughran, Campola, Tuffy Griffity and King Levinsky. Telegrams were received by Dempsey today from the managers of several of the fighters asking for details and declaring they would come here for the fight if satisfactory terms can be arranged. "We are shopping around right now for fighters," Dempsey said, "but expect no trouble in lining up a first-class card."

The fight will be held in an open-air ring in front
of the grandstand at the track and will start at noon. A
downtown office will be opened by Sacks within a day or
two to handle the details of the affair, he said.

The *Nevada State Journal* carried the story in its morning edition on
May 2 with a banner headline on page 1 reading "Dempsey Backs Heavyweight Bout Here July 4." The story carried the same details as that of the
Gazette, but added "it is also understood than an Uzcudun-Baer match would
be preferred by the promoters, could it be arranged." The matchup made
sense in terms of the potential crowd it could attract. Baer was an up-and-
coming fighter from the San Francisco Bay Area, whose nickname was the
"Livermore Butcher Boy."

Uzcudun, from Spain, was nicknamed "the Basque Woodchopper" and
Dempsey and his associates rightly surmised that Uzcudun would be popular
with the Basques in Nevada and surrounding states. In fact, they were counting on it. For the fight to be a success, it would have to draw visitors to Reno,
which had a population of just more than 27,000 in 1931. Uzcudun had
proven drawing power. When he fought in Los Angeles in early 1931, a large
contingent of Basques from Jordan Valley, Oregon and McDermitt, Nevada
made the drive south for the fight and they were hardly alone. Basques had
traveled from all over the west to cheer him on.

Uzcudun was the fighter Dempsey coveted most. Baer became more of
a risk on May 5, when he lost a 10-round decision to Johnny Risko in Cleveland. By May 8, Dempsey had had a series of telephone conversations with
Uzcudun and his manager, Lou Brix, in New York. (Brix had been one of
Gene Tunney's trainers when Tunny beat Dempsey for the title.) It was
agreed early on that Uzcudun would be coming, but there was a matter of
payment. He asked for either a guarantee of $12,500 and $1,000 for travel expenses or $10,000 and 30 percent of the gate. The negotiations were front-
page news in Winnemucca, where the *Humboldt Star* reported: "Basques in
Winnemucca today were joyous over the prospects of their countryman staging a battle in Reno and indications are that should the fight details be completed, an almost 100 percent exodus of his countryman here to the fight in
Reno will result."

Dempsey announced on May 9 that Uzcudun was signed for a 20-round
bout, though he didn't reveal the financial arrangements. He said the other
fighter would likely be Baer or Risko. That same day, in San Francisco, Ancil
Hoffman, one of Baer's managers, was telling newspapermen that Baer would
definitely be Uzcudun's opponent.

Promoters had some cause to be concerned about Baer, who, at 22, had as much of a reputation for being a playboy as he did for being a boxer. Newspapermen said that lately "Max had lost his punching power and his desire to battle" and that "too much night club stuff and too much sheiking was blamed."

Baer was in Reno on May 10, along with his managers J. Hamilton "Ham" Lorimer and Hoffman. They toured the Reno Race Track with Dempsey. Within a few days, Baer was signed and Reno's biggest fight since the Johnson-Jeffries heavyweight championship bout in 1910 was official.

Meanwhile, Dempsey and Leonard Sacks were suggesting that Reno could become a national fight center and the site of future heavyweight championship battles if the Fourth of July bout were a success. They set up official fight headquarters at 220 Virginia Street and Dempsey ordered all his office furniture and equipment from his headquarters in Chicago be moved to Reno.

On May 19, it was announced that training quarters had been selected for the two fighters. Baer would set up his camp at Lawton's Springs west of Reno and Uzcudun would establish his quarters at Steamboat Springs to the south of town. Uzcudun had originally wanted to use the facilities at Lawton's and had made long-distance arrangements to do just that, but Baer's team wanted them as well and signed the papers to use Lawton's during their visit to inspect the race track and sign on for the fight.

Uzcudun was reportedly steamed at Baer's actions and sent four telegrams to Dempsey. According to the *Reno Evening Gazette*, "In each one, he grew hotter under the collar. First, he charged Baer was no gentleman. Then he threatened to 'knock his block off' when the two got in the ring. In the last one, Paulino says he isn't going to wait for the July 4 fracas, but is going to 'start working' on Baer the first time he meets him in public after the pair get in Reno."

That same day of May 19, Dempsey caused a stir when it was revealed that he had ordered a training suit from San Francisco. Nothing sparked the interest of fight fans more than rumors of a Dempsey comeback. Dempsey admitted he'd be going through workouts at both training camps, but scoffed at the idea of a comeback. More likely, he wanted to make sure both fighters, and Baer in particular, were training hard for the fight. It was in his best financial interest to put on an entertaining show.

With the production in mind, Dempsey called in associates to help him prepare for the bout. They included Lloyd Stannard, his nephew, and George Brown to handle ticket sales and reservations. He also brought in Leo C. Owen, a veteran newspaper reporter, to handle publicity. Owen immediately announced that virtually all the top newspapermen from the West Coast would be attending the bout.

After brief discussions to lease land on the University of Nevada's farms fell through, construction of the arena at the racetrack began. Reno architect Frederick DeLongchamps was hired to design both the new clubhouse and the arena itself and work commenced quickly on both. Dempsey said the arena was being designed to seat 20,000 spectators and he expected it to be packed. He told reporters that in the first two days that the ticket office was open, more than 3,500 tickets had already been sold. Ticket prices ranged from $3 for general admission to $20 for ringside seats.

Dempsey ordered both fighters to be at their training camps a month prior to the Fourth of July and also took the unusual step of declaring that public admission to the training camps would be free of charge. In most big fights – Dempsey fights in particular – there was always a charge, but Dempsey was adamant. "Reno's thousands of daily visitors will want to take a look at Baer and Uzcudun during their month of training before the July 4 fight," Dempsey told the *Nevada State Journal*. "… We are trying to make the Nevada metropolis famous for its hospitality, so the usual admission charges will be done away with. Everybody will be admitted for free."

Ancil Hoffman made a brief stop in Reno on May 23 and offered up an exciting tidbit to reporters when he said he had "practically closed with Jack Johnson, former heavyweight champion of the world, to come here as Baer's sparring partner." Johnson had recently fought an exhibition in Southern California and would be a popular figure in camp. Hoffman did not mention that Johnson was 53 years old at the time. The deal apparently fell through as Johnson did not take part in Baer's camp.

Baer did show up earlier than Dempsey requested, and, was apparently serious about training and bursting with confidence. The *Nevada State Journal* was perhaps a little dubious from a story it ran on May 30 with the headline, "Max Bear Here for Training; Leaves Most of Suits at Home."

> Sans 38 of his 41 suits of clothes, but with his 16-cylinder car, his 'liveried chauffeur' and his 'social secretary' still along, Max Bear is back in Reno.
>
> Max was in Reno once before – but not for a grueling fight. He came here three or four months ago for a vacation. At that time, the big California heavyweight had on 36 suits of clothes, but Reno's pulchritudinous voted Max had no sartorial shortcomings despite his limited wardrobe.

The absence on this visit of Magnificent Max's seven trunks, however disappointing it might be to local divorcees-to-be, is eminently satisfactory to Jack Dempsey, who is sponsoring Baer's fight here on July 4 with Paulino Uzcudun.

Baer told reporters that he had actually only brought along two suits, the third outfit being a tuxedo, which he planned to wear to the Cal-Neva at Lake Tahoe or the Willows night club in Reno on the night after he beat Uzcudun. "I'm serious," he said. "No playing around for me from now until the fight is over. I'm going out and get that big Spiggoty quick! This is my big chance to get somewhere. If I snuff it, I might as well hang up the gloves. So I'm getting down to business."

Uzcudun, meanwhile, was running late and his manager, Lou Brix, informed Dempsey via telegram that the Basque fighter would not be arriving from New York until June 6. Part of the reason is that Uzcudun was waiting for the arrival of countryman Juanito Olaquibal from Spain. Olaquibal was a fellow heavyweight fighter and would be one of Uzcudun's primary sparring partners. Another reason was that Uzcudun planned to stay an extra day in Ogden, Utah, where "several thousands Basque residents of that vicinity will give him a huge reception and asked him to stay over a day and a night."

Indeed, Reno, and all the surrounding area where the Basques lived were excited for Uzcudun's arrival. A welcoming committee, headed by Martin Goni of Reno's Toscano hotel and restaurant, was established and it was determined that Goni would lead a contingent to Elko to meet Uzcudun on his way west. Celebrations were planned in Ogden, Elko and Winnemucca with a grand welcome in Reno.

As it turned out, Uzcudun did not stay an extra day in Ogden, preferring instead to get to Reno on the night of June 4 to get into training. He did make stops in all the cities as planned and was welcomed by hundreds of well-wishers along the way. The *Humboldt Star* newspaper in Winnemucca reported a huge crowd at the train station in anticipation of Uzcudun's arrival on Southern Pacific train No. 27. The paper also said Uzcudun was riding in car 80, drawing room D.

The train rolled into Reno after 11 p.m., where a brass band, Jack Dempsey and massive crowd packed the train platform. The *Nevada State Journal* reported his arrival in a mid-page story on its front page with the headline "Reno throngs cheer Uzcudun as big Basque arrives here."

Paulino Uzcudun, Basque woodchopper who will attempt to whittle down Max Baer, the walloping Californian, here July 4, literally piled 'em up when he caught his first view of Reno last night.

Uzcudun had difficulty getting a look at the city at all, and the thousands who crowded the Southern Pacific depot platform had just as much difficulty getting a look at Uzcudun.

The Basque heavyweight arrived on a Southern Pacific train shortly after eleven o'clock last night accompanied by an escort led by Martin Goni, Reno hotel man. Jack Dempsey, who is promoting the Baer-Uzcudun fight battle, was at the station.

The thousands who gathered to get a peep at the fighter from Spain found themselves crushed and jammed. They remained good-natured, however, and cheered at anyone who appeared at all as if he might be Uzcudun.

Flash lights blazed as photographers sought to secure snaps of the fighter and the crowds. "Uzcudun, Uzcudun, Uzcudun," cried a wailing voice in the back of the crowd.

The big Basque was escorted to the Riverside hotel by Dempsey and the latter's aides.

The lead story in the paper that day also concerned a key player in the July 4 event. Bill Graham, one of Dempsey's partners, was under investigation after he shot and killed gambler F. R. McCracken in Douglas alley. The story said a coroner's jury found the shooting to be in self-defense, however, there were calls for a grand jury investigation. From that day on, Graham's involvement with the Baer-Uzcudun fight went from the forefront to behind the scenes as only Jim McKay made public appearances with Dempsey.

At last, both fighters were in town and their training camps proved to be popular places with Reno's visitors. Hundreds of Basques trekked daily to Uzcudun's camp at Steamboat Springs, 10 miles south of Reno. Among them were the Laxalts of Carson City, father Dominique and his sons, Paul, the future Nevada governor and U.S. Senator, and Robert, who became an author. As Robert Laxalt recalled years later, "Jack Dempsey in his Reno days had tried to talk my father into giving up the sheep business to become a prize

Jack Dempsey, the No. 1 contender to the heavy-weight crown, was decked out in this Feb. 1919 photo in New York. *Colleen Rosencrantz Collection*

Jack Dempsey and Doc Kearns arrive in New York on Feb. 10, 1919 to sign for the heavyweight championship fight with champion Jess Willard. *Colleen Rosencrantz Collection*

An early Dempsey promotional photo taken in 1917. *Colleen Rosencrantz Collection*

Jack Dempsey shovels ore into a mining cart at the Champion's Mine in Midas, 1931. *Author's Collection*

Jack Dempsey strikes a pose, *circa* 1918. *Colleen Rosencrantz Collection*

A young Jack Dempsey in a pinstripe suit after winning the heavyweight championship of the world, *circa* 1920. *Colleen Rosencrantz Collection*

Jack Dempsey poses in a Los Angeles Angels uniform during the summer of 1923 when he was living in Los Angeles and making movies in Hollywood. *Colleen Rosencrantz Collection*

Heavyweight boxing champion Jack Dempsey attends a baseball game between the Los Angeles and Seattle of the old Pacific Coast League in the 1923 season. The young boy is Marty Krug Jr., next to his father, Los Angeles manager Marty Krug. Seattle manager Wade Killefer stands next to Dempsey. *Colleen Rosencrantz Collection*

Jack Dempsey gives boxing instructions to actor Rudolph Valentino, *circa* 1923. *Colleen Rosencrantz Collection*

Jack Dempsey poses with his
manager Doc Kearns, 1923.
Gary Schultz Collection

Jack Dempsey and Jack Kearns are
met by a rush of visitors, *circa* 1919.
Gary Schultz Collection

Dempsey made a minimum of $1,000 a week making films in Hollywood, *circa* 1920–25. *Colleen Rosencrantz Collection*

Jack Dempsey gets a ride in an airplane, *circa* 1920. *Colleen Rosencrantz Collection*

Dempsey and his training camp staff take a ride in Toledo, Ohio prior to his battle with Jess Willard, 1919. *Gary Schultz Collection*

One of Jack Dempsey's Hollywood co-stars was the "It Girl," Clara Bow, 1920–25. *Colleen Rosencrantz Collection*

Jack Dempsey poses with journalist J. D. Bannon, *circa* 1919.
Colleen Rosencrantz Collection

Jack Dempsey and Estelle Taylor in happier times in Los Angeles. They were divorced in 1931,
circa 1925.*Colleen Rosencrantz Collection*

A drawing of Jack Dempsey by artist
James Montgomery Flagg. *Colleen Rosencrantz
Collection.*

Jack Dempsey and newspaperman
Bob Edgren take part in a buffalo hunt,
1920–23. *Colleen Rosencrantz Collection*

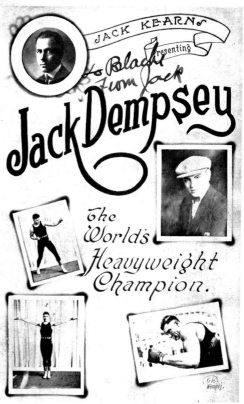

An early promotional postcard featured
Jack Kearns presenting heavyweight champion
Jack Dempsey, 1919. *Gary Schultz Collection*

Jack Dempsey stands over Georges Carpentier after knocking him out on July 2, 1921 at Boyles Thirty Acres in New Jersey. *Colleen Rosencrantz Collection*

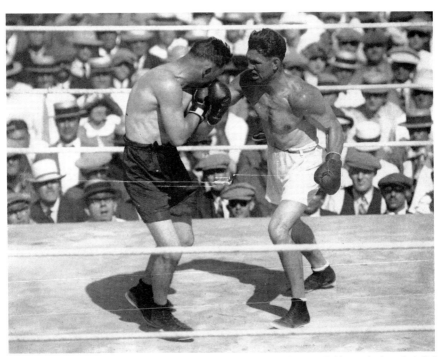

Jack Dempsey prepares to unleash a left hook at challenger Tommy Gibbons during their July 4, 1923 fight in Shelby, Montana. *Colleen Rosencrantz Collection*

Jack Dempsey poses with his mother during filming in
Hollywood. *Colleen Rosencrantz Collection*

Jack Dempsey poses with his parents, Celia and Hyrum Dempsey at his 1920 "slacker" trial
in San Francisco. *Colleen Rosencrantz Collection*

Jack Dempsey and his
mother, Celia, about 1920.
Colleen Rosencrantz Collection

Jack Dempsey portrait, early '20s.
Colleen Rosencrantz Collection

Dempsey poses during his championship reign, *circa* 1923.
Colleen Rosencrantz Collection

A young and dapper Jack Dempsey
poses for a photo, *circa* 1919.
Colleen Rosencrantz Collection

Jack Dempsey prepares for his title defense against
Bill Brennan in 1922. *Colleen Rosencrantz Collection*

Jack Dempsey prepares for his heavyweight championship bout with Jess Willard by taking on sparring partner Big Bill Tate, 1919. *Colleen Rosencrantz Collection*

Jack Dempsey and promoter Tex Rickard during Dempsey's championship reign, *circa* 1926. *Gary Schultz Collection*

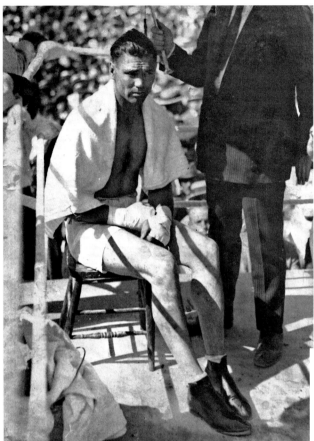

A reflective Jack Dempsey sits on a stool in the corner of the ring during his fight with Tommy Gibbons in Shelby, Montana, 1923.
Colleen Rosencrantz Collection

JACK DEMPSEY
CHAMPION OF THE WORLD
July 4, 1919 - Sept. 23, 1926

This photo of a young Jack Dempsey is displayed on a post card used by the Jack Dempsey Museum in Manassa, Colorado.

Dempsey strikes a pose in training for his 1926 fight with challenger Gene Tunney.
Reno Gazette-Journal File

Jack Dempsey shakes hands with his father, Hyrum, prior to the 1927 rematch with Gene Tunney.
Gary Schultz Collection

Dempsey, the sides of his head shaved, sits on a stool in his corner in one of his early title defenses, *circa* 1921. *Colleen Rosencrantz Collection*

Dempsey signed this photo of himself to his one-time promoter, Marius Durand, who owned the Mozart Club in Goldfield, *circa* 1930s. *Robert Quam Collection*

Dempsey spars with the Jamaica Kid, *circa* 1920. *Bill Pettite Collection*

Dempsey sits with a host of his sparring partners, including lightweight Pancho Villa, who sparred with Dempsey to help the champion prepare for his fight with smaller, quicker Georges Carpentier, *circa* 1921. *Gary Schultz Collection*

Postcards promote Dempsey's championship bout with Jess Willard and show his team of sparring partners, 1919. *Gary Schultz Collection*

Dempsey waits in his corner in the infamous long-count fight with Gene Tunney, 1927.
Reno Gazette-Journal File

Dempsey and Gene Tunney sign for their 1926 fight in which Tunney took the title from
Dempsey. *Colleen Rosencrantz Collection*

Dempsey poses with a pet dog in Reno during an unpublicized visit in 1929. *Gary Schultz Collection*

Jack Dempsey poses for a photograph during a visit to Reno in 1929. He often said he had mining interests in Nevada. *Gary Schultz Collection*

Dempsey poses on the steps of a Reno home during an unpublicized visit in 1929. *Gary Schultz Collection*

Dempsey sits in the California Avenue home he rented for $1,000 a month when he first relocated to Reno, 1931. *Gary Schultz Collection*

LAWN IN RENO GETS ATTENTION

Jack Dempsey does not believe in letting the grass grow under his feet. He is shown in the above photograph cutting the lawn at his home on California avenue in Reno. It helps keep him in trim, too.

The Nevada State Journal ran a photo of Dempsey mowing the lawn at his California Ave. home. *Reno Gazette-Journal File*

The Steinmiller-Parsons home on California Avenue is where Dempsey first stayed when he came to Reno to divorce actress Estelle Taylor. He rented the home for $1,000 a month. *Author's Collection*

Ham Lorimer   Jack Dempsey   Max Baer   Ancil Hoffman   Jim Mackay.
Max Baer - ... Inspecting Arena site at Reno Race Track ... April ... 4-14-31

Dempsey, second from left, examines the proposed Max Baer-Paulino Uzcudun fight site with, from left, Ham Lorimer, Max Baer, Ancil Hoffman and James McKay. *Colleen Rosencrantz Collection*

Dempsey poses with Bill Graham, Nevada Governor Fred Balzar and James McKay at the fight arena site. *Bill Pettite Collection*

Dempsey feeds a box of Cracker Jacks to a hippo, one of the animals in the Al G. Barnes Circus that visited Reno in May 1931. *Colleen Rosencrantz Collection*

Dempsey places his hat on a large hippo, part of the Al G. Barnes Circus that visited Reno in May 1931. *Colleen Rosencrantz Collection*

Dempsey poses with Jim McKay and an unidentified man after meeting the Al G. Barnes Circus in Reno in May 1931. *Colleen Rosencrantz Collection*

Dempsey prepares to feed a box of Cracker Jacks to a hippo, one of the animals in the Al G. Barnes Circus. *Colleen Rosencrantz Collection*

A banner across Virginia Street in downtown Reno advertises the Baer-Uzcudun fight on July 4, 1931. The fight headquarters is on the right. *Neal Cobb Collection*

Dempsey, standing, participates in the groundbreaking ceremony for his fight arena with Reno Police Chief Jack Kirkley, Reno Mayor E.E. Roberts, James McKay and Washoe County Sheriff Russell Trathen. *Colleen Rosencrantz Collection*

Jack Dempsey and James McKay stand with an unidentified man a the Reno Race Track. *Colleen Rosencrantz Collection*

Jack Dempsey breaks ground at the Reno Race Track for a fight arena. Looking on are Reno gamblers Bill Graham and James McKay. *Colleen Rosencrantz Collection*

Dempsey, center, stands with a group of youths from Susanville in May 1931. The visiting youngsters said meeting Dempsey was the No. 1 priority of their trip to Reno. *Neal Cobb Collection*

Jack Dempsey shakes hands with Reno Mayor E.E. Roberts after the groundbreaking event for Dempsey's fight arena. *Colleen Rosencrantz Collection*

Dempsey and his business manager, Leonard Sacks, take a seat at the Reno Race Track after the groundbreaking events. *Colleen Rosencrantz Collection*

Jack Dempsey and sportswriter Leo C. Owen, who Dempsey brought in to handle publicity for the Baer-Uzcudun fight. *Colleen Rosencrantz Collection*

Dempsey's business manager Leonard Sacks at Baer-Uzcudun fight headquarters. *Colleen Rosencrantz Collection*

Actor and wrestler Bull Montana, left, Paolino Uzcudun and Dempsey pose at Uzcudun's camp at Steamboat Springs, 1931. *Colleen Rosencrantz Collection*

Always popular with the kids, Dempsey poses with a pair at Uzcudun's camp. *Colleen Rosencrantz Collection*

Paulino Uzcudun, nicknamed "The Basque Woodchopper," spars with Jack Redmond. *Colleen Rosencrantz Collection*

Max Baer trains with a medicine ball at his camp at Lawton's Hot Springs in Reno. *Colleen Rosencrantz Collection*

LAWTON SPRINGS CAMP
JUNE -1931
HAM LORIMER   MAX BAER   ABE HUMPHREYS   ANCIL HOFFMAN

Max Baer clowns with his managers and trainers, Ham Lorimer, Dolph Thomas and Ancil Hoffman during training at Lawton Hot Springs. Colleen Rosencrantz Collection

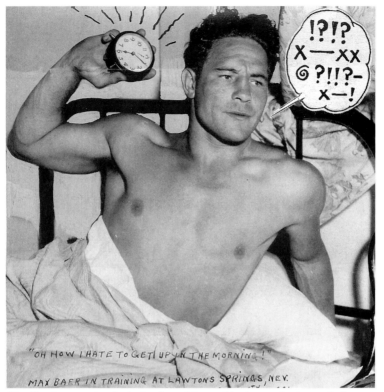

Max Baer's reputation for loving late nights and hating awakening early for training became the subject of jokes during his preparation for his bout with Paulino Uzcudun. *Colleen Rosencrantz Collection*

Nevada Gov. Fred Balzar, left, clowns with sportswriter and artist Bob Edgren Sr., and Bob Edgren Jr., referees, at Uzcudun's camp. *Colleen Rosencrantz Collection*

Paulino Uzcudun, former heavyweight contender Tom Sharkey, Dempsey and Bull Montana pose at Uzcudun's camp. *Colleen Rosencrantz Collection*

Dempsey was selected as the referee for the Baer-Uzcudun bout. *Colleen Rosencrantz Collection*

Jack Dempsey and Max Baer at Baer's Lawton Springs training camp. *Gary Schultz Collection*

JERRY LUVADIS   BARNEY DEMPSEY   PAULINO UZCUDUN   JACK DEMPSEY   MORRIE COHEN   LEONARD D SACKS
AT UZCUDUN'S CAMP - STEAMBOAT SPRINGS, NEV.
JUNE 20 - 1931

Jerry "The Greek" Luvadis, Bernie Dempsey, Paulino Uzcudun, Dempsey, Morrie Cohen and Leonard Sacks pose with two unidentified men at Uzcudun's training camp. *Colleen Rosencrantz Collection*

Paulino Uzcudun takes on the role of chef as he enjoys a barbecue with his fellow Basques at his training camp at Steamboat Springs. *Colleen Rosencrantz Collection*

Dempsey spars with Al Gomez at Uzcudun's camp at Steamboat Springs. *Colleen Rosencrantz Collection*

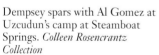

Jack Dempsey presents flowers to Mrs. Kyne, wife of Reno Race Track owner, William Kyne at the Reno train depot. *Colleen Rosencrantz Collection*

Jack Dempsey congratulates the winner of the Jack Dempsey Handicap horse race held on July 3, 1931. *Nevada Historical Society*

№ 379

GENERAL LICENSE

COUNTY OF
WASHOE
NEVADA

1931

NOT TRANSFERABLE

$ 100.00   RENO, NEVADA, MAY 20, 1931

RENO RACING ASSOCIATION -JACK DEMPSEY-PROMOTER having paid to the License Collector of Washoe County the sum of ONE HUNDRED Dollars, is hereby entitled to conduct a PRIZE FIGHT business at RENO RACE TRACK ON for~~~~~~~~~~~~~~ JULY 4th , 1931, in conformity with and subject to the provisions of law.

A.W.Dunkle
County Treasurer

Della B. Boyd
County Auditor

RECEIVED PAYMENT IN FULL ON ABOVE LICENSE

By _W.J. Ferguson_ Deputy.   Sheriff.

Dempsey paid $100 for a license to hold the Baer-Uzcudun fight. *Colleen Rosencrantz Collection*

The Jack Dempsey Arena, built for the Baer-Uzcudun bout, stands completed at the Reno Race Track. *Colleen Rosencrantz Collection*

The crowd starts to fill the 15,000-seat Jack Dempsey Arena for the
Max Baer-Paulino Uzcudun fight on July 4, 1931. *Colleen Rosencrantz Collection*

More than 15,000 fans fill the seats under a blistering July 4 sky at the Jack Dempsey Arena for the
Baer-Uzcudun fight. *Neal Cobb Collection*

More than 15,000 fans fill the seats under a blistering July 4 sky at the Jack Dempsey Arena for the Baer-Uzcudun fight. *Colleen Rosencrantz Collection*

Max Baer, left, and Paulino Uzcudun flank Jack Dempsey prior to the start of their July 4, 1931 fight. Also pictured are Nevada Gov. Fred Balzar and Lt. Gov. Morley Griswold. *Colleen Rosencrantz Collection*

Max Baer, left, and Paulino Uzcudun flank Jack Dempsey prior to the start of their July 4, 1931 fight. *Colleen Rosencrantz Collection*

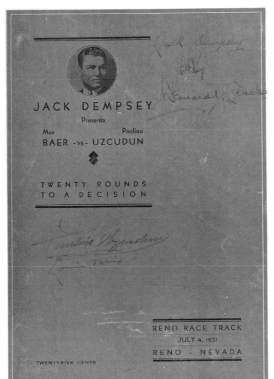

The program for the Baer-Uzcudun fight featured a photo of Jack Dempsey on the cover. *Colleen Rosencrantz Collection*

Max Baer, facing camera, and Paulino Uzcudun battle in their 20-round bout at the Jack Dempsey Arena on July 4, 1931. *Colleen Rosencrantz Collection*

Paulino Uzcudun, left, and Max Baer battle in their 20-round bout at Jack Dempsey Arena. Dempsey is the referee. *Colleen Rosencrantz Collection*

Jack Dempsey poses for a publicity photo at the Reno Boxing Club, later known as the Chestnut Street Arena, in August 1931. He signed the photo to Lt. Gov. Morley Griswold. *Bill Griswold Collection*

Jack Dempsey stands in the Reno Boxing Club with his trainer, Jerry Luvadis, left, and business manager Leonard Sacks. *Colleen Rosencrantz Collection*

Jack Dempsey poses with Ernie Evans, Dick Evans, Max Baer, Max Evans (front) and casino executive Harold Smith during a visit to Reno in the mid-1950s. *Jim Pace Collection*

The interior of the Eastside Inn included large photos of Jack Dempsey and Dick Evans, *circa* 1950s. *Evelyn Pace Collection*

.FILE NO. 54574.

STATE OF NEVADA, } ss.
County of Elko, }

MARRIAGE CERTIFICATE

344

I, J. A. McFarlane, Justice of the Peace

of the County of Elko, State of Nevada, do hereby certify that in the ~~town~~ City of Elko

County of Elko, State of Nevada, on this 18 day of July A. D. 19 33, I united in

Marriage JACK DEMPSEY of WASHOE County,

STATE OF NEVADA and HANNAH WILLIAMS

of WASHOE County STATE OF NEVADA and that the said Marriage was

with their mutual consent

solemnized in the presence of Mike Cantwell and Maurice E. Cain

who were witnesses.

Witness my hand this 18th day of July A. D. 19 33

Mike Cantwell
Maurice E. Cain } Witnesses.

J.A.McFarlane

Justice of the Peace

Filed for record at request of J.A.McFarlane,J.P. on the 7th day of August A. D. 19 33,

at 9:05 o'clock A.M.,

Wm.Rigsby County Recorder.

The marriage license for Jack Dempsey and Hannah Williams, who were married in a surprise ceremony at the Elko County Courthouse, 1933.

Sincerest
NEW YEAR
GREETINGS

BARBARA · JOAN
JACK DEMPSEY

Jack Dempsey's Holiday Card features him in his U.S. Coast Guard uniform flaked by his daughters, Joan and Barbara, 1944. *Colleen Rosencrantz Collection*

Jack Dempsey listens to Las Vegas Sun publisher Hank Greenspun, right, interviews gambler Nick "The Greek" Dandelos, 1950s. *Las Vegas Sun File*

Jack Dempsey pretends to spar with former heavyweight Jack Van Noy as brothers Ernie, left, and Dick Evans look on at the Evans brothers Eastside Inn in Reno in 1964. *Evelyn Pace Collection*

Jack Dempsey receives a cowboy hat from Ernie Hall, exalted ruler of the Elko Elks Lodge, in February 1961. Dempsey was the keynote speaker at the annual Youth Night event in Elko. *Northeast Nevada Museum and Historical Society*

Reno casino owner Nick Abelman, a friend of Jack Dempsey since 1915 in Goldfield and Tonopah, stands with his son, Bob, at the Jack Dempsey Casino at the Reno Race Track in 1931. *Bill Pettite Collection*

Photos of Jack Dempsey through the years show him at ages 21, 32, 50, 66 and 75. *Reno Gazette-Journal file.*

Jack Dempsey is flanked by business partner Ancil Hoffman and Reno native Bill Pettite at a birthday celebration for Hoffman, the longtime manager of Max Baer, 1969. *Bill Pettite Collection*

Jack Dempsey pretends to deliver an punch to the jaw of Reno native Bill Pettite. Pettite would drive Dempsey from Sacramento to Reno to visit friends, 1969. *Bill Pettite Collection*

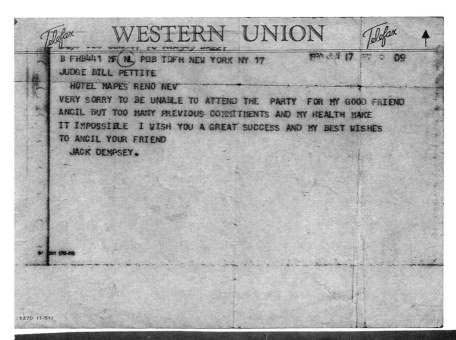

WESTERN UNION *Telefax* *Telefax*

B FHB441 NF NL PDB TDFH NEW YORK NY 17   1970 JUN 17 PM 0 09

JUDGE BILL PETTITE

HOTEL MAPES RENO NEV

VERY SORRY TO BE UNABLE TO ATTEND THE PARTY FOR MY GOOD FRIEND
ANCIL BUT TOO MANY PREVIOUS COMMITMENTS AND MY HEALTH MAKE
IT IMPOSSIBLE I WISH YOU A GREAT SUCCESS AND MY BEST WISHES
TO ANCIL YOUR FRIEND

JACK DEMPSEY.

---

western union   **Telegram**

1970 JUN 17 PM

1970 JUN 17   1970 JUN 17 PM 3 48

1001A PDT JUN 17 70 PRA113

SYA176 SY WSA069 BA NL PDF TDWS SCARSDALE NY 17

JUDGE BILL PETTITE DLY 75

EXECUTIVE OFFICE HOTEL MAPES RENO NEV

DEAR JUDGE

IT IS WITH DEEP REGRET THAT WE CANNOT BE WITH YOU ON THIS MOST
IMPORTANT DAY TO CELEBRATE WITH YOU AND TO PARTICIPATE IN THE
GOLDEN DAYS OF BOXING BANQUET AND TO PAY TRIBUTE TO OUR DEAR
PAL ANCIL HOFFMAN ON HIS 86TH BIRTHDAY GOD BLESS FOR MANY MORE
YEARS WE SALUTE YOU BILL FOR YOUR UNTIRING EFFORTS AND TO CHARLES
MAPES FOR HIS DEVOTION AND WE SALUTE ALL OUR DEAR FRIENDS AND
PALS WHO WILL BE HONORED ON THIS MEMORABLE OCCASION GOD BLESS
ALL OF YOU WITH EVERY GOOD WISH SINCERELY

JACK DEMPSEY AND DAVE MARGOLIS.

Telegrams sent from Jack Dempsey to Bill Pettite express Dempsey's regret in not being able to attend a birthday celebration for Ancil Hoffman planned in Reno in 1970. *Bill Pettite Collection*

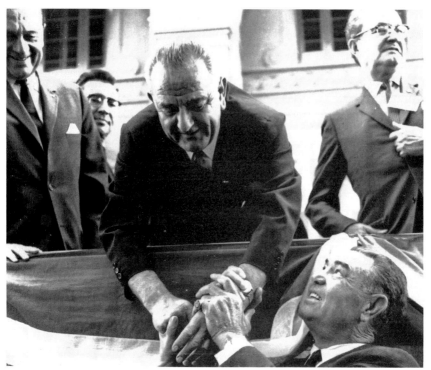

President Lyndon B. Johnson shakes hands with Jack Dempsey during a campaign stop in Reno on Oct. 12, 1964. Johnson spoke to an estimated crowd of 20,000 at the State Building. Also pictured are Nevada U.S. Sen. Howard Cannon, Gov. Grant Sawyer and U.S. Sen. Alan Bible. Dempsey was in Reno awaiting his fourth wife's divorce from her first husband to become final. *Neal Cobb Collection*

Jack Dempsey holds hands with his fourth wife, Deanna, at their New York apartment in 1977. The couple spent six weeks in Reno in 1964 awaiting Deanna's divorce from her first husband. *Reno Gazette-Journal File*

fighter; we practically lived at Steamboat Springs near Reno when Paulino Uzcudun, the Basque woodchopper, was training for his bout with Max Baer.

Baer's camp was equally popular, especially with the "pretty blonde members of the divorce colony." Baer's promise to focus on training and not on fun apparently hit a snag after a little more than a week. That's when he received a terse, three-page letter from Dempsey with a list of do's and don'ts for the remainder of his training period. According to newspaper reports, Dempsey said Baer "could not use or even ride in his own automobile, could not go horseback riding, could not parade around Reno in off-training hours in fancy clothes." In addition, Baer was to put himself "under the domination of his trainer, Dolph Thomas."

Baer's reaction to the letter was one of anger. "Jack's letter to me is hardly justified," he told reporters. "Whoever has been telling him I was not training seriously for the fight is an outright liar. I was never more serious in my life. And Jack needn't worry – just on account of that letter, I'm going to plaster Upsidedown (Uzcudun) all over that ring."

The *Nevada State Journal* reported that the letter had its intended impact on Baer as on June 13, he "cut loose with a vengeance on his five sparring partners who were thrown into the ring with him."

Uzcudun, meanwhile, was a wildly popular figure at his camp at Steamboat Springs. On June 14, members of the Reno Moose Lodge and surrounding lodges held a picnic and barbecue in his honor at the training camp. "Not less than 1,000 people are expected to watch Paulino train this afternoon," the *Journal* reported. "Eats will be served starting at 1 p.m. and Paulino will start his training workouts about 2:30." The jovial Uzcudun took part in the barbecue, slicing meat for the well-wishers.

Dempsey became a frequent visitor to both camps, often donning his training tights and working on the heavy bags or going a couple of rounds with sparring partners of Baer and Uzcudun. One afternoon, he tangled with wrestler Bull Montana to the delight of the crowd. On another occasion, his training suit was stolen at Baer's camp and Baer saved the day by offering the former champion one of his spare outfits.

Dempsey was also busy promoting the fight. He made a quick trip to Los Angeles to ensure many of his Hollywood friends would be coming. A few days later, he was back in Reno for the announcement of a new airline service between Reno and Los Angeles on Gilpin Air Lines that would include extra flights for the Fourth of July weekend, exclusively for those planning to attend the bout.

Dempsey also made a trip to Winnemucca along with Governor Fred

Balzar, state Senator Noble Getchell, state engineer G. W. Malone and Jim McKay and was honored with a banquet by the local American Legion post, Vernon Robinson Post 5. They were to leave Reno in the morning on June 23 and arrive in Winnemucca about 4 p.m. A scare went through the city when dispatches from Los Angeles inquired about an accident in which a party headed by Dempsey had been seriously injured or killed. The rumors proved unfounded when Dempsey's party rolled into town at 3 p.m. Dempsey borrowed a line from another famous one-time resident of Nevada when he quipped to reporters, "the reports of my death or injuries are greatly exaggerated."

After a banquet at the Humboldt Hotel, Dempsey gave details of the Baer-Uzcudun fight, saying, in his opinion, Max Baer would win the bout if it were held that day. Still, he urged all Winnemucca residents and all the area Basques to turn out in support of Uzcudun.

Reno city leaders, meanwhile, were scrambling to ensure the throngs of visitors expected for the Fourth of July celebration would have a place to stay. Arrangements were made with the railroad to bring extra Pullman cars in which visitors who didn't have a room reservation could sleep. In addition, the Chamber of Commerce asked homeowners with extra rooms to make them available for visitors, telling residents this was Reno's golden opportunity to show visitors it was a friendly city.

Tickets for the fight were selling well. In fact, they were selling a little too well as it turned out. Two men were arrested in Reno for counterfeiting tickets to the fight and selling them to unsuspecting visitors. Simultaneously, police officials in San Francisco and Oakland were looking for three men who had been attempting to sell counterfeit tickets. Dempsey quickly issued a statement after admitting he had heard rumors of counterfeit tickets, but discounted them. "We want to protect the public in every way possible," he said. "If purchasers will cooperate with us and buy their tickets only from authorized sales agencies in San Francisco, Oakland, Los Angeles and other large cities, they run no risk of getting counterfeits."

In the two weeks before the fight, the training camps became so popular that Dempsey waived the no-charge policy he had imposed earlier and fans were charged a quarter to attend. A stir at Uzcudun camp occurred when Dolph Thomas, one of Baer's trainers, was discovered in the crowd, intent on "getting a line on the Basque," newspaper reports said. "After discovering Baer's trainer trying to 'spy' on the Basque, everybody expected to see Thomas manhandled and rushed pell-mell from the camp – with a couple of Uzcudun's huskies accelerating the progress," the *Nevada State Journal* reported. "Instead, Lou Brix, manager of Paulino, sought out Dolph and voluntarily showed him everything in the camp and then insisted that they have afternoon lunch together. The last seen of Dolph, he was sipping tea, or some other amber-colored fluid, with Paulino's manager."

By July 1, Reno was filling up and the crowd continued to swell as the weekend approached, the Fourth of July falling on a Saturday. Horse races – including the Paulino Cup, Max Baer Cup and Jack Dempsey Cup – were held at the racetrack in the days before the race, all attracting record crowds.

Visitors were arriving by planes, trains and automobiles. In fact, highway officials were predicting the most use ever of the highway between San Francisco and Reno. Southern Pacific Railroad announced 10 special trains would be coming to Reno filled with fight fans – four from San Francisco, two from Los Angeles to carry the Hollywood contingent, one from Salt Lake City filled with "Jack Dempsey's friends", one from Klamath Falls, Oregon and others from San Jose and Vallejo. Another train carrying Elks club members from Detroit would detour to Reno on its way to a convention in Seattle so the members could take in the fight.

Betting was heavy with Uzcudun a slight favorite because of the large amount of money being bet by his fellow Basques, who were streaming in from all points throughout the west.

Baer and Uzcudun might have been the principals in the fight, but the star of the production was clearly Jack Dempsey. Hollywood newspaperman and novelist Jim Tulley might have summed it up best when he spoke a at a dinner for Uzcudun that featured several Hollywood stars, sportswriters and other dignitaries, "I came to watch Jack Dempsey referee," he said. Indeed, on the day before the fight, the lead headline in the *Reno Evening Gazette* read: "Dempsey and His Fighters All Set To Entertain Crowd of 15,000 at Fistic Carnival at Track Tomorrow."

Dempsey had covered all angles to ensure a large crowd. With Uzcudun, he drew the Basque crowd. With Baer, he attracted interest from the Bay Area. With the undercard including Sparks' own Tony Poloni, who had won the national amateur championship in June, he secured plenty of local interest. And by himself, Dempsey drew a crowd, including Hollywood stars Edward G. Robinson, the Marx Brothers, Tom Mix, Buster Keaton and W.C. Fields. Sports stars included boxers Tony Canzoneri, the reigning lightweight and junior welterweight champion; former heavyweight contender Tom Sharkey; and Willie Ritchie, former lightweight champion; billiards players Willie Hoppe and Welker Cochran; and retired baseball stars Big Bill Lange and Ty Cobb, the Georgia Peach himself.

Dozens of the top sportswriters from the West Coast were in town to cover the fight, including Harry B. Smith of the *San Francisco Chronicle*, Russell J. Newland of The Associated Press, Mark Kelley of the *Los Angeles Examiner*, Pat Frayne of the *San Francisco Call-Bulletin*, Tom Laird of the *San Francisco News*, Curley Grieve of the *San Francisco Examiner*, Steve George of the *Sacramento Union* and John Cahlan, a Reno native who was working for the *Las Vegas Review-Journal*. Cahlan recalled in his oral history years later that this was his first opportunity to meet Dempsey, but they would later form a partnership on a pair of Las Vegas boxers.

Even on the fight program, Dempsey was the star. While Baer and Uzcudun were named on the cover, the only photo was of Dempsey. Dozens of Reno businesses advertised in the program, most with notes that said "Good luck to Jack Dempsey and his fighters." (An advertisement for Steamboat Hot Springs touted its "radio-active" waters.)

On the second page of the program, Dempsey paid tribute to the man who had first put Reno on the map as a fight center. The page featured a photo of the late Tex Rickard and this note from Dempsey:

> "In the promotion of this event I have endeavored, and I hope not unsuccessfully, to complete the unfinished labors of my friend and pal, George L. "Tex" Rickard.

JACK DEMPSEY

Others that Dempsey recognized in the program were Fredrick DeLongchamps, architect for both the fight arena and the clubhouse; the Clover Valley Lumber Company, which provided the lumber for the arena and the arena contractor J.C. Dillard.

Fight officials included timekeepers William Justi and Senator "Wild Bill" Lyons; official weighers Sanford C. Dinsmore and George Murphy; official physicians Vinton A. Muller and Horace J. Brown; announcers Dan Tobey and Buzz White; head ticket manager George H. Brown; publicity chief Oscar Otis; accountant Lloyd Stannard; office personnel Ann Penson and Gertrude Thornton; and official photographers Ray Howard, Charles Orr, J.B. Scott and Roy Curtis.

Potential referees for the undercard bouts included Reno's Frankie Neal; and Lt. Jack Kennedy of Los Angeles. Dempsey was the referee and sole judge for the Baer-Uzcudun fight, which was scheduled to begin at 12:30 p.m. and go 20 rounds.

Reno Police reported cars lining up and heading for the arena at 2 a.m.

and Reno Police Chief Kirkley took personal charge of the traffic squad. By the start of the preliminary bouts at 10 a.m., the $3 general admission seats and the $5 reserved seats were nearly filled and the crowd swelled as the main event approached. The temperature swelled as well, nearing 100 degrees by noon. An estimated 15,000 people packed into the stadium with 3,000 more taking to the grandstands of the racetrack for a far-off view, however one that was shaded from the sweltering sun. The summer of 1931 was one of the hottest in Reno's history. In fact, it was the hottest on record until 2005. The freshly cut pine board that was used in building the arena was still green and pitch boiled out of it and onto the clothes of patrons. One youngster sitting in the stands that day was Ty Cobb (no relation to the baseball player), who wrote about the experience years later while a columnist for the *Reno Gazette-Journal*:

> I attended the fight with my uncle, Will Harris. The tickets were $5 but we moved down when some were opened closer to the ring. The arena was specially constructed out of new pine boards. Under the roasting July sun, pitch soon oozed out of the new planks. My new slacks, costing about $4.50, were ruined and my mother chewed me out when I got home.

The *Reno Evening Gazette* described the scene this way:

> Braving a burning sun and the discomforts of blistering pine board seats that oozed pitch, Reno and its legion of visitors turned out in numbers to help Jack Dempsey in his first promotional venture here. The former heavyweight champion was the busiest man in the place, shaking hands with friends, showing others to their seats and generally filling the duties of a "Handy Andy."

After all the ballyhoo leading up to the fight, the main event itself proved to be a solid, though unspectacular display. Both Baer and Uzcudun went into the fight confident and both declared they would score a knockout. The 5-foot-11 Uzcudun said his strategy was to pound away at the 6-foot-2 Baer's body and chop the bigger man down. Baer had never been 20 rounds, he said, while Uzcudun had fought several 20 round bouts in Europe. Baer told reporters, "I think I'll belt the big mug out of the picture, maybe in the 11th or 12th round." He said he planned to counter whatever punch Uzcudun threw his way.

Promoter and referee Dempsey, who had heard rumors earlier in the day that a fix was in for the bout, drew both fighters together for their instructions. "Boys, I've heard that this fight is fixed. I know nothing about it, but this I do know. If at any time this fight looks fishy or either one of you tries to lay down, the fight will be stopped and both your purses cancelled."

Uzcudun followed his game plan from the start, working hard lefts to the body. Baer countered, but often swung wildly when he saw openings. In the sixth, Uzcudun had Baer in trouble, but the Californian recovered and by the eighth round, he was landing the majority of blows as Uzcudun retreated around the ring. Baer's confidence grew and he was reported to be smiling and winking at his corner men – and at a divorcee named Dorothy Dunbar, who was sitting at ringside. (Baer and Dunbar were married four days after the bout, the final blow in Baer's relationship with his manager Ham Lorimer.)

But Uzcudun recovered and the fighters spent the remainder of the bout slugging it out under the blazing sun with neither fighter gaining a huge advantage or scoring a knockdown. If the fix was in, it was forgotten by the two combatants. As the *Nevada State Journal* described it, "A couple of wildcats could hardly have been more vicious than the two warriors who violated most of the rules of ring etiquette in efforts to beat each other down into the resin of the sun-scorched battle pit."

After 19 grueling rounds, referee Dempsey announced whichever fighter prevailed in the 20th round would be declared the winner. The veteran Uzcudun continued his body attack and dodged Baer's sweeping blows. After the final bell, Dempsey raised Uzcudun's arm in victory, much to the delight of the thousands of Basques in attendance.

Questioned by reporters later that evening as he hosted a party for an estimated 50 celebrities, Dempsey called the fight a success and was already looking ahead. The fight had grossed an estimated $100,000. Uzcudun's purse was $18,000 and Baer's was $12,000. "I promise you there will be another major fight in Reno for Labor Day," Dempsey said. "I wouldn't make such a promise if I was disappointed in the outcome of today's 20-round battle."

What Dempsey didn't say, probably because he didn't know it at the time, was that he would be the star attraction on Labor Day.

Maybe it was his workouts in the training camps or perhaps it was standing in the ring, even as a referee, and hearing a cheering crowd of thousands. Maybe it was his friends and manager urging him on. Whatever the case, a fire was burning in Dempsey's belly to step back into the ring with his chin tucked and his fists blazing.

13
'Our Jack'

In early August of 1931, Leonard Sacks announced that Jack Dempsey would be starting a "pugilistic tour" at mid-month, and, if all went according to plan, it just might prompt another challenge for the heavyweight championship. The tour would be starting in his adopted hometown of Reno on August 19 at the new Reno Boxing Club. The *Nevada State Journal* carried a page 2 story under the headline "Manassa Mauler Ready to Storm Boxing Heights."

> The great Manassa Mauler, Jack Dempsey himself, will crawl back through the hemp barrier as a prize fighter on August 19 at the new Reno Boxing Club if Joe Dillard and Frankie Neal are able to find an opponent for him, said his manager Leonard Sacks.
>
> For the past 30 days, the man who thrilled millions during his spectacular ring career which included 78 matches and the heavyweight championship of the world has been training hard in preparation for a pugilistic tour which will start in Reno and end in the east.

The story explained that the tour would start in Reno and take Dempsey to the Pacific Northwest, Idaho, Montana and then points east. He would fight four-round battles and would be paid $5,000 per appearance, plus half the gate. Sacks said more than 100 cities had already expressed interest in hosting the former champion.

So at 36 year old and 217 pounds – and nearly four years after his last fight – Jack Dempsey was back in training. His typical workout consisted of

12 rounds – three on the light bag, three on the heavy bag, three rounds of shadow boxing and three rounds of boxing or calisthenics. By mid-August, he was tipping the scales at 199 pounds. Promoters Joe Dillard and Frankie Neal were able to line up not one, but two opponents for Dempsey: Jack Beasley of Oakland and Tony Fuente of Old Mexico.

On the Friday before the Wednesday night fight, Dempsey sparred five rounds with four different opponents, including Leo Hansen, "who gave the champion a very active round and had Dempsey covering up most of the time." Explained *Nevada State Journal* reporter Jim Newlands: "His work with Dempsey was to polish off the man killer's defense." Dempsey spent the next round trying to get through the defenses of Tommy Smith and followed that with a round against Jerry Rooney. Then came two rounds with Big Bill Hartwell, a black fighter from Boston, who was also scheduled to be one of Dempsey's opponents in Portland a few days later. Hartwell, "never laid an effective piece of leather on the former champion and left the ring bleeding from the mouth," Newlands wrote. "It was apparent that Dempsey could have stowed him away any time he pleased."

"Our Jack" DEMPSEY

During Dempsey's comeback tour, the Reno newspapers featured him in advertisements for a Labor Day bout, referring to him as "Our Jack" Dempsey. *Reno Gazette-Journal File*

Before his comeback could begin, Dempsey did have one bit of unfinished business to take care of: his divorce from Estelle Taylor. On August 17, just two days before his Reno fight, he appeared in the Second Judicial District Court in Reno with his attorney, Robert E. Burns, and residency witness James McKay, with a complaint charging Taylor with "extreme cruelty." Judge Thomas F. Moran presided over the hearing and ordered a summons be hand-delivered to Estelle Taylor in Los Angeles or posted in the *Reno Evening Gazette* "once a week for four weeks." Dempsey chose the former, and a man named B.J. Cunningham personally served Taylor with the complaint the same day. Moran scheduled a hearing for September 21 in his court. One day after receiving her summons, Estelle Taylor filed for divorce in Los Angeles and Dempsey was ordered to appear on August 27.

After all his court battles – from the slacker trial to the dozens of lawsuits filed by Jack Kearns – Dempsey wasn't about to let these become a distraction. They certainly weren't a distraction for the Reno press, which had bought into Dempsey's comeback lock, stock and barrel as shown by this advance story by Jim Newlands in the *Nevada State Journal* on the morning of the fight:

> It is the belief of one popular songwriter "The World is Waiting for the Sunrise" but not in Reno. In this capital of the sagebrush world they are waiting for tonight and the official return of Jack Dempsey to the squared circle he deserted some three years ago after being robbed of his crown in Chicago to "the long count."
>
> The old battle horse of all the pugilistic heavy-weight aspirants will take up his fighting career tonight at the New Reno Boxing Club before the greatest in-door crowd to ever assemble here. Jack Beasley and Tony Fuente have been picked as his opponents. Dempsey is the heavy favorite to cop both decisions in two rounds or less.
>
> In spite of the matrimonial entanglements, tonight the champion of champions will be back in the ring. And if he is worried over the impending court actions Reno fans will never know it. Tonight he will be the Manassa Mauler again and what he does in Reno, the sporting world will know tomorrow. If the good wishes of Nevadans count for anything, Jack Dempsey will again be crowned "King of the Heavyweights."

Newlands certainly wasn't the only Reno citizen in Dempsey's corner. The arena was packed on fight night despite the fact that Tony Fuente, and a third fighter, Ray Pelkey, backed out of battling Dempsey at the last minute. Upon entering the ring, a smiling, waving Dempsey received "the greatest ovation ever accorded a fighter here," the *Journal* reported. Governor Fred Balzar also entered the ring and he, Dempsey and Beasley posed for photographer Roy Howard. The fight itself lasted barely longer than the photo shoot.

In the first round, Dempsey contented himself to work on defense, blocking most of the blows Beasley attempted to deliver, although the champion did take "a few stiff cracks to the whiskers, which bothered him little, if at all." Beasley did seem willing to mix it up, however.

The end came quickly in the second round. Dempsey came out in his familiar crouch and a scowl appeared on his face. He closed in and whipped a left hook to the side of Beasley's head and the challenger went to the canvas. He arose at the count of nine and Dempsey closed in, whipped another left to Beasley's head and put him down again. For a second time, Beasley was up at nine, but another left put him down and out.

Fans wanted more, so after Beasley was revived, he was offered "an additional cash remuneration" and agreed to another go. When he was counted out early in the third round, he declined a similar offer to go a fourth, citing illness. Newlands summed up his opinion of the fight this way:

> It was a great start for a great fighter in his honest
> effort to recapture the throne he lost to Gene Tunney.
> It is doubtful that anyone at the New Reno Boxing Club
> last night doubts his ability to win the coveted title.

The reaction of the Reno crowd certainly left an impression on Dempsey's handlers, who announced two days later that Dempsey would headline a Labor Day weekend card at the race track arena. His manager, Leonard Sacks, told reporters that Bill Graham had guaranteed Dempsey $10,000 for a four-round bout. An opponent hadn't been secured, but it was announced that Les Kennedy would be approached to take on Dempsey.

Dempsey had left Reno a day after the fight, driving to Boise. He was said to be planning a short stop in Winnemucca to visit friends before going on to the Idaho city where he would take the Union Pacific to Portland for battles with four fighters in the same night. Two days after that, he was in Seattle to face three opponents and two days later he was in Vancouver, British Columbia to take on three more challengers. Three days later, he was in Spokane and knocked out four fighters – Elgin Taylor, Dee Richmond, Tony Talerico and Cyclone Thompson – all in the first round.

He was on the coast in Aberdeen, Washington two days later and scheduled for a fight in Eugene, Oregon two days after that. Tragic news caught up with him as he made his way to Eugene. His brother Bernie, who had battled lung disease for years, had passed away in Los Angeles. Dempsey told reporters he was shocked at the news. "I have always looked up to Bernie. He was my oldest brother and is responsible for my having started in the fight game. In fact, for a time in the early stages of my pugilistic career, he was my advisor and manager. Bernie loved the fight game. It was his first love. He never missed the opportunity to impart to a youngster whatever he thought might be helpful advice."

Dempsey said his first impulse was to cancel the bout in Eugene and his scheduled Labor Day battle in Reno, but said it wouldn't have been fair to the promoters or to the fans that had bought tickets to see him.

Reno, meanwhile, had been readily preparing for Dempsey's Labor Day bout. A parade was planned on Virginia Street with three bands, a military color guard, Governor Fred Balzar and the mayors of Reno and Sparks all scheduled to participate. Both the *Reno Evening Gazette* and *Nevada State Journal* were running full-page advertisements for the weekend's festivities, complete with a pen-and-ink drawing of Dempsey with the caption "Our Jack" Dempsey below it. Reno had claimed Dempsey as its favorite son.

Everything, it seemed, was set – with one big exception. It was still unknown whom Dempsey would be fighting. A week earlier, it was anticipated that Dempsey would face Leo Lomski, the Aberdeen Assassin, in a four round bout. But Lomski pulled out two days before the fight, leaving Dempsey without an opponent and no doubt causing a case of panic for promoters. Programs for the bout were printed showing Dempsey on the cover and four question marks in the place of an opponent's name.

At some point, organizers decided to seek all comers to battle Dempsey in two-round exhibitions that would serve as the wind-up to a 10-round main event featuring Sparks light heavyweight Tony Poloni against Tommy Bennett of San Jose. Sacks said Dempsey would fight "any three men who have the intestinal stamina to enter the ring against him. In fact, he will go further than that and fight all five of the present candidates if they arrive at the ring ready for action. The five candidates being considered were Hans Birkie, Tom Sawyer, Sailor Jimmy Flinker, Sam Baker and Eddie Burns. Birkie, called the "German heavyweight sensation from the Pacific Coast" was rumored to be holding out for more money to battle Dempsey. In the end, Eddie Burns, Sam Baker and Bob "Red" Tingley were selected as Dempsey's opponents.

Upon his arrival in Reno, Dempsey also took the opportunity to call his grieving mother and assure her he would be in Salt Lake City for his brother's funeral. After his bouts in Reno, he was scheduled on the 9:30 p.m. train and would be in Utah the following afternoon.

He could have taken an earlier train.

A crowd reported to be 14,000 – 10,111 in paid attendance – filed into the arena for the Labor Day fight program. It was cloudy and a slight breeze gave fans a little discomfort. The good news was the pine bench seats that oozed hot pitch during the Baer-Uzcudun battle had dried out in the four-plus months since the arena was built.

The card opened with a battle between the Diaboldt brothers, one calling himself "Young Dempsey" and the other "Young Tunney." They fought to a draw. Joe Horton, a former Nevada amateur, came next, scoring a knockout over Sacramento's Jerry McCrae in the second round. The third fight featured Jimmy Quilici of Smith Valley taking a four-round decision over Dempsey's one-time sparring mate Jerry Rooney.

Two more undercard fights followed before Dempsey entered the ring to enthusiastic applause. Main event or not, most of the fans had clearly come to see Dempsey in action. Newlands' report of the fight was somewhat subdued. Perhaps he had used up all his superlatives in his preview stories. Here's how the *Journal* had it the following day:

> For his first opponent, the former heavyweight champion toyed with Eddie Burns of Davenport, Iowa. Dempsey took both rounds against the Iowan with ease. Jim Gifford of San Francisco was the third man in the ring.
>
> Following Burns into the ring came Sam Baker of Douglas, Ariz. His visit with the Manassa Mauler was of very short duration and he succumbed to a smash to the midriff. He was apparently so badly hurt that he couldn't stand up – that is, until he was counted out.
>
> Dempsey's final opponent was Bob Tingley of Seattle who was ballyhooed as having fought Tony Poloni to a draw. He didn't come even close with Dempsey and was dropped twice in the opening stanza with lefts to the chin. The second round was a repetition with Tingley bouncing to the canvas three times.
>
> The former champion, in his final round with Tingley, snapped into a lively waltz and gave the fans many laughs when he repeatedly grabbed his redheaded adversary to keep him from sliding into the resin. It was the best of the three exhibitions and was well worth the price of admission and the trip.

Later that night, Dempsey was on the train headed east for Salt Lake City. He wouldn't be out of state for long, however. He had to be back in Reno later in the month to finalize his divorce. Then he was planning to take an extended break for a little light training, some sagehen hunting and perhaps a little gold mining on the side.

14
'Renovated'

On September 21, 1931, a Monday, Jack Dempsey was back in Reno after a hectic two-week period that took him from the Labor Day bouts in Reno to his brother's funeral in Salt Lake City, to exhibitions in Tacoma, Washington; Rock Springs, Wyoming; Salt Lake City; Logan, Utah; and Boise Idaho. He was ready for a break, but not before finally taking care of the matter that had brought him to Reno in the first place – his divorce from Estelle Taylor.

Dempsey, his lawyer Robert E. Burns, and James McKay, appeared in Department 1 of the Second Judicial District Court with Judge Thomas F. Moran presiding. Estelle Taylor did not respond to the summons for her to appear and did not attend the hearing in Reno. Burns' first order of business was to submit a request that "all papers, records, proceedings and evidence including exhibits and transcript of the testimony … be sealed and not opened to anyone except the parties hereto, or their attorneys." Whether Judge Moran denied the request at the time or at a later date, the transcripts of the trial ended up in the public records of Washoe County, case number 36675.

The trial opened with Moran reading the case number and taking another request from Burns.

"Before proceeding with this case, Your Honor, I move that the Court exclude everybody from the court room."

Moran responded: "All right, that will be the order."

James McKay was sworn in as the first witness and Burns began questioning. McKay answered five questions in 10 words and was dismissed from the stand.

Q: Are you familiar with the plaintiff in this action, William Harrison Dempsey?

A: I am.

Q: Did you see William Harrison Dempsey in Reno, Washoe County, Nevada on April 11, 1931?

Jack Dempsey is flanked by his divorce lawyer, Robert Burns, left, and his residency witness, James McKay, on the steps of the Washoe County Courthouse after securing his divorce from Estelle Taylor in August 1931. *Dan Bennett Collection*

A: I did.

Q: From the 11th of April to and including the 17th day of August, did you see Mr. Dempsey in Washoe County, Nevada each and every day?

A: I did.

Q: And you know of your own knowledge that he was present in Washoe County, Nevada each and every day between those dates?

A: I do.

Q: Does Mr. Dempsey own property in the state of Nevada, Mr. McKay?

A: He does.

Burns: That is all.

Jack Dempsey was next to take the stand, perhaps a little nervous because he misspoke when Burns asked him when he arrived in Reno.

"On March 11, 1931," Dempsey testified.

"I beg to correct you on that," Burns said. "Are you not mistaken – was it not on April 11, 1931."

"April 11, 1931," Dempsey responded.

Like McKay, Dempsey responded to Burns' questions of residency with two-word answers and he kept his answers equally brief until asked to establish his reasons for claiming "extreme cruelty" in seeking the divorce.

"I have been connected with the fight game since I was sixteen years old and before Mrs. Dempsey and I were married, we had an agreement that after we were married, she was to make one or two pictures and then give up her career as an actress and I was to continue in the fight game," Dempsey testified. "She did this for a while and soon after she began taking part in motion pictures, which I objected to. She nagged at me and quarreled with me and found fault, and criticized my friends, especially my friends in the fight game."

"This continued from a few months after we were married practically every week until 1929."

Later in the testimony, Burns asked Dempsey why he objected to his wife continuing her career as an actress.

"I wanted her to settle down and have a home and go with me wherever I went. She objected to this, and she said she thought more of her career than anything, and she would never leave Hollywood and go with me."

Dempsey went on to testify that he and Estelle had essentially split up in 1929 and in April of that year, she had requested he deed her their home in Hollywood as a property settlement. Dempsey did so.

He said after the property settlement, Estelle's attitude toward him was cold and hostile and in March of 1931, when he tried to visit her in Hollywood, she brushed him off, repeatedly, choosing instead to go out on the town with her friends.

"I went to her room and asked her what she meant by not having met me, and by staying out for our five nights, and she told me that I knew what it meant, that she was all through with me, she said. 'You and I have our settlement, and this is my house and if you don't get out and stay out, I will get the policemen to put you out' and I said 'You cannot mean that', and she said, 'I was never more serious in my life', and I said 'Very well, I will pack my clothes and get out.'"

Burns went on to ask Dempsey how Estelle's actions made him feel.

"It made me miserable," Dempsey said.

"What effect did all of this conduct to which you have testified, have upon your health?"

"It made me very nervous and affected my health."

"Did it destroy your happiness and and peace of mind?"

"It did."

"Did her conduct defeat the ends and purposes of the marriage?"

"It did."

"Do you feel there is any possible chance of a reconciliation being effected between yourself and your wife?"

"Absolutely none."

Burns concluded his case by asking that the 1929 property settlement be admitted into evidence. Moran granted the request as Plaintiff Exhibit 1. Dempsey was excused from the stand and Moran took no time before delivering his judgement.

"Judgment for the plaintiff and against the defendant, granting to the plaintiff a decree of divorce dissolving the bonds of matrimony now and heretofore existing between William Harrison Dempsey, Plaintiff, and Estelle Taylor, Defendant, and restoring said parties to the status of unmarried persons."

Jack Dempsey signed the appropriate papers with his given name, "William Harrison Dempsey," probably one of the few times in his adult life that he used something other than "Jack Dempsey."

His second tumultuous marriage was finally over – he'd been "Renovated" as the national press liked to say. He was eager for a little rest – away from Hollywood and wide-open Reno – and the opportunity to get a little more serious about his comeback.

He certainly sounded serious in an interview with Phil Sinnott of the Newspaper Enterprise Association two days after his divorce hearing. "I'm out to regain the world's heavyweight championship, just as determined and just as confident as I was before I beat Willard at Toledo twelve years ago," Dempsey said. "And I'm not doing a comeback because I think I can. I know I can after these so-called 'exhibition bouts' in which any opponent would clip your chin any old time he could land on it."

Dempsey scoffed at the idea that he was too old, at 36, to regain the title. "I'm thirty-six and in a few months, I'll be a 'perfect 36'. Bob Fitzsimmons was thirty-five when he won the title. And he had to buck one of the greatest generations of heavies the world will ever know."

Dempsey said with his legal and marital woes behind him at last, he was mentally ready to return to the ring with a vigor. "This mental hazard cost me my title," he said. "I'm going to get my title back and my mind's at peace."

He was ready to go back to his roots, the hard physical conditioning that started in the mines of Colorado and the lonely railroads and mining camps of the West. To borrow a modern phrase, Jack Dempsey wanted to go old school and he knew just where to go to do so – a place right in the heart of Nevada.

15
A Gentleman in Midas

"There have been a thousand and one things I enjoyed doing in my life, but the two things I enjoyed most were fighting and mining," Jack Dempsey said in his 1959 autobiography.

It was those two pleasures that led Dempsey to the small northern Nevada mining camp of Midas, population 130, in the fall of 1931.

Dempsey was no stranger to the town when he arrived for a month-long stay in September of 1931. In late July, with the Baer-Uzcudun fight concluded, he accompanied Noble Getchell, who had just bought mining claims in Midas, on a trip there for the opening of sagehen hunting season. They had traveled by car from Reno, stopping in Lovelock for lunch before driving on to Battle Mountain where Getchell "took great pleasure in introducing Dempsey to his many friends and acquaintances." Getchell represented Lander County in the state legislature and owned the *Battle Mountain Scout* newspaper. They had dinner at the Parker Come As You Are Inn before driving south for the night to the mining camp of Betty O'Neal, where Getchell had a home.

They were back in Battle Mountain the next morning before making their way north to Midas where they were joined by their hunting partners: Nevada Governor Fred Balzar, California Governor James Rolph and Matt Penrose, warden of the Nevada state prison. As locals tell it, the hunting party had a grand time and were perfect gentlemen, Dempsey in particular.

"Mrs. Getchell asked Dad if I could come over and help her serve and wash dishes," recalled Noreen Murdock in an oral history of Midas. "She was cooking for Jack Dempsey, Governor Balzar, and the governor from California and Warden Penrose from the prison. (Because) I was just a kid, they'd all get in there and help me do dishes and clean up and serve or whatever. They were just the neatest bunch of men, as I remember. And then at night it would be dark, of course, when I'd get through and go home. I got Jack to walk me home. He was a real neat guy."

The area was rich with sagehen, mule deer and other game. It also had some other attributes that caught Dempsey's attention. Midas itself was at an elevation of 6,000 feet – just about the same level as Lake Tahoe – and the nearby peaks climbed to more than 8,000 feet. For an athlete looking to get in tip-top shape, it was a perfect training ground.

No doubt, that was in Dempsey's mind when he entered a partnership with Getchell, Jim McKay and Tex Hall in mining properties in Midas. The Macy Mine, as it was named when Getchell bought it, was located at the top of Water Canyon at more than 8,000 feet in elevation. It was renamed the "Champion Mine" in Dempsey's honor and simply called the Dempsey Mine by locals.

In late August, as Dempsey was on the first leg of his comeback tour, the partnership was announced in northern Nevada newspapers. When Dempsey arrived back in Reno for his Labor Day bout, his manager, Leonard Sacks announced that Dempsey would head for Midas near the end of the month for several weeks of training.

Getchell quickly went to work to prepare the mine and a training quarters, complete with an outdoor ring, for Dempsey's arrival. He contracted with three mining men, Max Mashner, Jerry Paul and Clayton Byer, to dig the first 100 feet of the planned 500-foot tunnel. Getchell told the Reno newspapers, that Dempsey would not be digging in the tunnel because he didn't want the champion exposed to the powder fumes and dead air. Instead, Dempsey would help in building a road to the tunnel portal. The Winnemucca and Battle Mountain newspapers, however, both reported that Dempsey would be "making the dirt fly" in the tunnel.

Dempsey's headquarters were set up in the Gold Circle Consolidated Company's office and a ring was erected next to the office building. "His trainer and sparring partner, also his cook, are on the ground," the *Reno Evening Gazette* reported. "Jack is scheduled to take a regular shift on the 'Armstrong hoist' in order to strengthen his back, and to do much road work and mountain climbing."

On the afternoon of September 23, Dempsey departed Reno for Midas in the company of Joe Vincent, a Salt Lake City friend, and Vincent's family, which included his wife, their daughter, LaVon, and granddaughter. They checked into the Hotel Humboldt in Winnemucca, where Getchell joined the group that night, and left for Midas at 8 a.m. the following morning. The *Humboldt Star* newspaper caught up with Dempsey before his departure and described the scene.

> Dempsey was found in the lobby of the Hotel Humboldt this morning with the little Vincent child in his arms, apparently enjoying himself immensely. The child, a little blonde tot with blue eyes, was landing rights and lefts to Dempsey's face, much to her own amusement and to Dempsey's. It was only with much encouragement that Mrs. Vincent persuaded the child to leave Jack.

Jack Dempsey stands between Nevada State Sen. Noble Getchell, left, and trainer Jerry Luvadis while training at the Nevada mining camp of Midas. *Author's Collection*

Some of six or seven local residents seated in the lobby gave evidence of Dempsey's present place in the spotlight of sports. Their eyes were without exception glued on the ex-champ.

Dempsey appeared in excellent condition, slightly thin as a result of training, but not haggard or worn out. He still looks comparatively young and plenty able to get back that crown which he lost to Gene Tunney several years ago.

In Midas, Dempsey made himself at home. He even brought in some greyhound dogs, which he used to hunt coyotes in nearby Squaw Valley. In the mornings, he would run from the office building several miles to the mine and in the evenings, he would run back. He would also spend time shadow boxing and sparring in the ring where the Midas townfolk could watch him work out.

Dempsey was a popular figure in town. While he had a well-deserved reputation as a fierce competitor in the ring, outside the ring, he was friendly, polite, playful and generous. He even took time to play a little jump rope with some of the children in town.

Edna Timmons recalled being home in Midas from high school in Reno and cooking for Dempsey and his group. When they learned she was heading back to school, they each pitched in and gave her $25.

Near the end of his stay, the town threw a dance in Dempsey's honor. In the Midas oral history, resident Gordon Warren said it had to be a record crowd at the community hall that night.

"Well, I think the largest crowd that I ever saw there was (for) what they called the Dempsey Dance," Warren said. "They had this dance and you couldn't get anywheres near it, there were so many people. … Just crushed if you got inside."

Dempsey made sure to dance with all the girls.

He continued his training in Midas until October 8 when he returned to Reno. The *Reno Evening Gazette* reported his arrival on October 10. "He will remain here until October 19, he said today, keeping in training the whole time, and then go to Salt Lake and the Jackson Hole country for a few days, and then back east to resume his barnstorming appearance."

On October 14, Dempsey purchased a home in Reno, a seven-room brick house in the Newlands Manor subdivision, from Lena Dormio. The *Gazette* said the house had been built only a few months earlier and the sale price was $14,000.

Three nights later, Dempsey refereed a wrestling match between Peter Visser and Tommy Thompson at the Chestnut Street Arena (formerly the Reno Boxing Club) and then he was back on the road, this time joining Getchell, Balzar, Joe Vincent and several others on a big-game hunting trip to Jackson Hole, Wyoming. As with virtually anything Dempsey did, his exploits on the hunting trip made the newspapers. The *Reno Evening Gazette* reported it this way on October 27:

> Jack Dempsey and Noble H. Getchell, senator from Lander County, were the only two members of the Nevada hunting party who secured moose during their recent hunt in Wyoming, according to word received from Dempsey today from Salt Lake. Apparently Governor Balzar and other members of the party did not get their moose.
>
> According to the Salt Lake report, Dempsey brought down a twelve hundred pound moose with three shots. Getchell's was a bit smaller. Following the hunt, Governor Balzar went to Portland, Ore., while the balance of the party, with the exception of Dempsey, returned home.

Dempsey headed to Salt Lake City with Joe Vincent after the hunt. He played a little golf, relaxed and visited his mother. In early November, a story appeared in the *Miami News* in Florida that Dempsey had given LaVon Vincent a ring. LaVon Vincent was Joe Vincent's daughter and the mother of the child Dempsey was clowning with in the Hotel Humboldt in Winnemucca. She issued a statement that appeared in the *Reno Evening Gazette* and other papers on November 4 that denied the Miami story. "I'm just a friend of Jack's, like the rest of my family," she said. "There is no engagement and no romance."

The only ring Dempsey was concerned about was the boxing ring. He resumed his comeback on November 6 against three fighters in Provo, Utah then headed east to Des Moines, Iowa and points east that he hoped would lead him to another shot at the world's heavyweight championship.

Jack Dempsey prepares for a training session at the Reno Boxing Club, later known as the Chestnut Street Arena. Trainer Jerry Luvadis helps him into his gloves. The photographer misidentified Luvadis as "Sacks" in the writing on the photo. Leonard Sacks was Dempsey's business manager, 1931. *Nevada Historical Society*

16
Realization

Between August 18, 1931, when he launched his comeback with a second-round knockout of Jack Beasley in Reno, and the end of the year, Jack Dempsey fought 62 times. He made thousands of dollars at each appearance, a far cry from the million-dollar gates of the 1920s, but a nice chunk of change nonetheless. He often fought two, three or four men in the same night and generally scored a quick knockout or won by decision. He was 36 years old, but was feeling good in the ring and getting encouragement from his handlers.

In January of 1932, he was back in his home base of Reno and talks were under way for his comeback to become serious and for Reno to be the center of it. Playing a key role would be James McKay, who accompanied Dempsey on much of his 1931 exhibition tour. On Jan. 11, 1932, the *Reno Evening Gazette* ran a story under the headline: "Pugilisitc Come-Back Effort of Jack Dempsey May Place James McKay in Rickard's Place."

> If the first half of Jack Dempsey's come-back is successful, pugilistically and financially, will the McKay Syndicate of which James McKay, local sportsman, becomes a factor in national boxing activities?
>
> That's a question being asked now and the answer is probably yes.
>
> Everything depends, of course, on Dempsey's ability to defeat Primo Carnera or some other heavyweight

in the battle that is scheduled to be held here on July 2. If Dempsey wins the Reno fight, he will be in direct line to meet Max Schmeling, the champion, and will be, next to Schmeling, the outstanding fighter of the world with greater box office pull than Schmeling or any other two celebrities.

The story went on to say that McKay was ready to step into the void left by the death of Tex Rickard as the preeminent fight promoter in the country. It added that Dempsey's services would be in such demand, if he won in Reno in July, that he could simply demand that he would only fight if McKay were the promoter.

Dempsey did that for Rickard a few years ago. He was the big card of Rickard's stable and the former Nevada gambler rode to fame on Dempsey's boxing ability. Dempsey would fight for Rickard any time and would pay little attention to other promoters.

McKay's friends say the Nevada sportsman is not adverse to stepping into the national sporting arena and prospective million dollar contests and is willing to risk his reputed wealth in the venture. He has much more money than Rickard had when he broke into the game in a big way and he is even a closer friend of Dempsey than was Rickard during the early days of Rickard's big time promotions.

McKay's "personal wealth" didn't stop his group from reaching out to Reno businesses and unions for financial help in securing the July fight. A businessman's committee was formed to build financial support for the endeavor and auto dealer John C. Durham was named chairman. Other members were Ken Foster, Harry Stewart, John Mueller, Phil Gilson and H. C. Heidtman. On Jan. 23, the businessman's group, plus Dempsey, Governor Fred Balzar and Mayor E. E. Roberts, met with a large contingent of union members at Hutton's Hut (known today as Johnny's Little Italy) on West Fourth Street. Dempsey, despite suffering from a bad cold and fever, gave a short speech, calling the union members "brothers and sisters" since he, too, held a union card. Dempsey explained he had been a member of the Western Federation of Miners in Colorado in 1910 and was later a member of the Boilermakers Union in Seattle. He also said he was a member of "a Reno local" and that he was "behind union labor 100 percent."

J. B. Clinedinst, president of the Painters Union, presided over the meeting and introduced the procession of speakers that included prominent lawyer William Woodburn who told the crowd that "with farming and mining depressed, the only chance for Reno's continued prosperity was to bring thousands here during the spring and summer, and this, he said, the big fight would do. ... There is no greater attraction in the country than Jack Dempsey."

Balzar implored the crowd to support Dempsey, who he called "the stellar attraction of the nation, greater than even the President. He likes Reno. He wants to be one of you. Don't let him get away." Durham spoke next, saying the fight would be assured with labor's help.

The union leaders were obviously convinced. By a unanimous vote, representatives of the 37 unions, agreed to form a committee to work with the businessman's committee to help promote the fight. Within a few weeks, $15,000 in cash and $35,000 in pledges were secured from Reno businesses and unions.

That done, Dempsey went back on the road. On Feb. 1, he knocked out Bad News Johnson in three rounds and Wally Hunt in one round in Stockton, California. He then headed east to Milwaukee, winning two-round decisions over Buck Everett and Jack Roper on Feb. 8. Three days later, he knocked out K.O. Christner in three rounds in Cleveland and three days after that, in Flint, Michigan, he dispatched George Kohler and Pat McLaughlin with first-round knockouts.

Victories were coming easy. As Dempsey put it: "The ham-donnies I was fighting were falling over like tenpins. Boxing writers were saying – at least the younger ones were – that I was hitting as hard as I had hit nine years before, the night I got paid $120,000 a minute for belting Firpo for a little under four minutes."

Dempsey and his handlers felt it was time to step up the class of boxers he was facing to see if what the writers were saying was true. And so the stage was set, as the *Nevada State Journal* explained in a February 18 story written by United Press Staff Correspondent George Kirksey under the headline: "Dempsey At Cross Roads Of Comeback: Future Rests on Result of Levinsky Bout."

> Jack Dempsey reaches the cross-roads of his comeback campaign (tonight) when he meets King Levinsky, Chicago's clouting clown, in a four-round exhibition bout in Chicago Stadium.

The result will determine whether Dempsey is
through as a first-class fighter or whether he has a
chance to beat back along the comeback trail that was
too tough and treacherous for Jim Corbett, Bob
Fitzsimmons, Jim Jeffries and Jess Willard.

In meeting Levinsky, Dempsey emerges from the
"soft touch" league for the most important test he has
faced since he began his exhibition tour at Reno, Nev.,
last August. Levinsky is ranked No. 7 among the heavyweights by the National Boxing Association.

While Kirksey explained the stakes, he also added his own opinion of
the former champion's chances against the 21-year-old Levinsky. "Not only
does Dempsey still have plenty of dynamite in both fists, but, at 36, more
than five years after he lost his title to Gene Tunney, he remains the greatest
attraction in the boxing game."

Kirksey was certainly right about the "greatest attraction" part. More
than 20,000 fans bought tickets in advance for the exhibition fight with
Levinsky at the indoor Chicago Stadium. An additional 4,000 general admission, standing-room-only tickets were made available the day of the fight and
most of them were quickly snapped up. In all, a record crowd of 23,322 attended the exhibition, with hundreds forced to sit in the aisles or stand on the
runways. The gate was $74,199 – far behind the million-dollar gates of the
1920s that Dempsey attracted, but an impressive total for a non-judged fight
in the height of the Great Depression.

As with most Dempsey fights, there was no lack of action from the
opening bell to the finish – actually beyond the finish because the two fighters
were exchanging blows after the final bell. Kirksey, described each round:

Levinsky Is Hurt

In the first round, Dempsey hurt Levinsky several
times with body punches and had the 21-year-old
Chicago fish-peddler's body red.

Levinsky fought clumsily in the opening round,
frequently fanning the air with wild hooks which passed
harmlessly over Dempsey's crouched head.

Draw in Second

After winning the first round, Dempsey got no
better than an even break in the second round. Once or

twice he landed short left hooks which made Levinsky go into retreat, but the King, younger and fresher, landed more blows.

Levinsky won the third round, hurting Dempsey several times with punches to the head. Dempsey actually had to go on the defensive, bobbing and weaving to get out of the path of Levinsky's wild hooks.

Both Are Tired

Both fighters were tired when they came out for the fourth round. Dempsey kept boring in, throwing short punches to the midsection and taking everything Levinsky could give to the head in return.

Dempsey's left hook seemed very ineffective in this round and he unloosed it only a few times at Levinsky's head.

The final tally of the 24 newspapermen at ringside: 18 for Levinsky; 2 for Dempsey; 4 for a draw. Kirksey's conclusion: "Dempsey, making his first appearance in a Chicago ring since he knocked down Gene Tunney for the famous '14-count' in Soldier Field in September 1927, failed to show anything to warrant hopes for his staging a successful comeback."

The *New York Times* was more blunt. It's lead paragraph on the story read: "Jack Dempsey's pugilistic come-back ran into a stone wall tonight."

The *Nevada State Journal* was much more sympathetic on its editorial page the following day, running an item with a headline reading, "Don't Be Upset."

Don't be upset over the results of the encounter between Jack Dempsey and King Levinsky in Chicago last night.

Judging from the number of telephone calls received by The Journal last night, Reno has more Dempsey fans per capita than any other community in the country.

And all the folks who inquired by telephone about the fight results expressed disappointment over the draw given the Reno man in his battle with the Chicago clown.

Of course, Levinsky is no pushover. He is No. 7 heavyweight of the country.

Dempsey was not in proper condition.

Jack left Reno a month ago with an attack of the flu. He fought in Stockton despite his condition.

Since then, he has been jumping from place to place, meeting a couple of local heavies in each town.

It takes a couple of months of steady training, regular living, regular meals and regular sleeping to get in condition for a fight with the recognized No. 7 heavyweight fighter of the country.

But Dempsey has not had regular sleeping, regular meals and practically no training.

And, at that, Levinsky was unable to slow down Dempsey or hurt him.

After his loss to Levinsky, Dempsey fought 17 more exhibitions in the following six weeks to fulfill contractual obligations and then headed for Reno in early April. Sacks and McKay were vowing that the bout between Dempsey and Carnera still was in the works for the Fourth of July and from there a fight with Jack Sharkey was inevitable.

Dempsey just sounded relieved to be back in Reno.

"I'm just going to loaf for a month," he told the *Reno Evening Gazette* on April 9. "Well, maybe I'll take a bit of a workout now and then – but mostly just lazing around. I have a slight cold, but feel okay otherwise. Glad to have the rest after barnstorming the country for so many months. Boy, this is home to me – home sweet home."

Dempsey knew in his heart his boxing career was finished. He wrote of it years later in his autobiography and called the fight with Levinsky "a lucky thing."

Kingfish Levinsky slapped me all over the ring in four rounds. I knew it was time to hang them up for keeps. If I had ever been sap enough to get in there with Sharkey, (who took the title from Schmeling in June 1932) at thirty-seven, he probably would have knocked me out, and that would have been no way to end a career.

Jack Dempsey's comeback in search of the heavyweight championship was over.

17
Politics, Rodeos and Romance

As Leonard Sacks and Jim McKay were working on another fight for Dempsey in the spring of 1932, another old Nevada friend – state Sen. Noble Getchell – was looking at Dempsey for a different type of battle – one that Getchell hoped would help Herbert Hoover stay in the White House.

Dempsey owned a house on Joaquin Miller Avenue in Reno and Getchell – probably at the urging of George Wingfield and Governor Fred Balzar – came to the conclusion that Dempsey would be an outstanding delegate for Nevada at the Republican National Convention later in the year. Under the headline: "From Fighter To Politician: Or the Rise of G.O.P. Delegate J. Dempsey", the *Nevada State Journal* announced the savvy political move by Getchell.

> Jack Dempsey, who has never registered or voted, is being boomed for delegate to the Republican National Convention in Chicago next June. Jack was recently elected delegate to the state convention from the Mount Rose School precinct.
>
> Democrats gnashed their teeth when they heard about the Republican coup, believing "first come, first served," and the party that had the bright idea first would have been the chosen party for the pugilistic champ.

> Noble Getchell, chairman of the Nevada state cen-
> tral committee, announced Friday an invitation would
> be extended to Dempsey to be a member of Nevada's
> delegation to the Republican National Convention.

James G. Scrugham, the former Nevada governor, was editor of the *Nevada State Journal* at the time and also said in an editorial that the only reason Dempsey wasn't with the Democrats is because the Republicans got to him first. Scrugham happened to be running as a Democrat for the U.S. House of Representatives and would win the seat in the November election as Democrats swept to a landside victory.

Apparently Dempsey's plan to "loaf around" Reno for a month wasn't entirely accurate as Getchell also announced on April 22 that he would be heading for Los Angeles to extend the GOP's invitation to Dempsey. Dempsey loved Hollywood and the social scene. Single since his divorce from Estelle Taylor, he was a regular in the gossip columns. He explained it in his 1977 autobiography: "In that period of my life, I must have been linked with everyone in a skirt. Sure, I screwed around, and so did everyone else I knew. But I wasn't as intense as the press made me out to be. One woman, Follies dancer and film actress Lina Basquette, almost got me into hot water. She was said to be my ex-trainer Teddy Hayes' girlfriend when she decided to take up with me. She was a beautiful woman and I was flattered. … Lena and I were together for a while in Reno."

There were even rumors Dempsey and Basquette were married. Basquette married nine times in her life, but never to Dempsey. She also was the favorite actress of Adolph Hitler, who invited her to Germany for a visit in the 1930s.

Whether Dempsey turned down Getchell's offer that week in Los Angeles or changed his mind at a later date, he wasn't a Nevada delegate at the 1932 Republican convention. The Republicans nominated Hoover, the incumbent, who lost in a landslide to Democrat Franklin D. Roosevelt. A few years later when Dempsey did become politically active, he was a strong supporter of Roosevelt and his New Deal policies, and appeared at a number of campaign rallies for Roosevelt.

His loss to Levinsky certainly didn't hurt Dempsey's popularity in Reno. He was in constant demand to speak at the service clubs and to lend his name to all sorts of endeavors. That spring of 1932, the city planned to resurrect its rodeo celebration that had been defunct after going bankrupt a decade earlier. Community leaders including Charles J. Sadleir, the manager of

Jack Dempsey holds a trophy, known as the "Jack Dempsey Trophy" that was presented to the saddle bronc riding champion at the 1932 Reno Rodeo. Dempsey is standing in front of the home he purchased on Joaquin Miller Avenue in Reno. *Bill Griswold Collection*

George Wingfield's Riverside Hotel, and Harry Drackert, a cowboy who became a divorce ranch owner, brought the rodeo back to life.

Dempsey participated in the rodeo by lending his name to the championship trophy in the bronc riding event. The large silver cup had a boxing figure on top and horse heads carved around the base. Dempsey, duded up in a western hat and scarf, posed for a photo with it outside his Reno home. Canadian cowboy Pete Knight, who went on to win the 1932 world championship in saddle bronc riding, won the Jack Dempsey Trophy. The trophy survives today at the National Cowboy and Western Heritage Museum in Oklahoma City.

18
Baer-Levinsky

E ven if his comeback had officially ended – in his mind at least, if not the minds of his manager and promoter – Jack Dempsey was a busy man. Throughout May and June of 1932, he was back and forth between Reno and Los Angeles a number of times, often in the company of Lina Basquette, though sometimes on his own or with his manager, Leonard Sacks. On May 4, after a few days of workouts at the Chestnut Street Arena, he left for Modesto to referee a fight. He then planned a quick trip to Oakland before heading to Los Angeles for the opening of the Jack Dempsey Grill at the corner of Sixth Street and Westlake Boulevard. Dempsey also owned the Barbara Hotel in Los Angeles that was managed by his brother, Joe.

After two weeks in Los Angeles in which he denied rumors about a reconciliation with Estelle Taylor, Dempsey started making his way back north toward Reno. He had agreed to referee bouts in San Bernardino, San Jose and San Francisco before returning to Reno at the end of the month. In mid-May, stories began appearing in Reno newspapers intimating that offers were being made to Max Baer and Kingfish Levinsky for a July bout in Reno. All the while, Sacks insisted he was still trying to secure a big-name opponent for Dempsey.

On May 25, Sacks and Jim McKay announced that Levinsky and Baer would battle for 20 rounds on July 4 and Dempsey would not be fighting. John C. Durham of the Reno businessman's committee announced the $50,000 raised to secure the Dempsey bout would be returned "dollar for dollar" at once. Dempsey returned to Reno with Sacks the following day.

The *Nevada State Journal* took note in its May 27 edition:

> Jack Dempsey and his manager, Leonard Sacks, returned to Reno from San Francisco last night full of plans for the July 4 battle between Harry K. Levinsky of Chicago and Max Baer, the butcher boy from Livermore, Calif.
>
> It's going to be a great battle, with a card of preliminaries which will make the entire promotion the year's big sports event of its kind on the western slope.
>
> Levinsky and his sister, Mrs. Lena Levy, who is also his manager, will arrive here June 1. Sacks said last night Baer is due in the Lake Tahoe neighborhood today and will arrive in Reno Tuesday.
>
> Both Levinsky and Baer will do their training here, in camps yet to be selected. Ancil Hoffman, Baer's manager, will arrive in Reno Tuesday.
>
> Dempsey himself is going to get down to some serious training, Sacks said last night. He will alternate between the two camps. It is possible, said Sacks, that Dempsey may take on the winner of the July 4 battle in September and the location of such an encounter will be Reno.

Jim McKay announced plans to expand the Dempsey Arena at the racetrack to accommodate between 25,000 and 35,000 spectators – up from the 15,000 of when it was built the year before. He also said a fence would be installed around the facility to keep spectators from sneaking in as they had for Baer-Uzcudun.

Baer, who had already been training at Lake Tahoe, came to Reno two days later and selected Lawton's Springs for his training camp and the Mayberry Dude Ranch for his living quarters. He also stopped by the Washoe County courthouse to file divorce papers against Dorothy Dunbar, the woman he had married in Reno a few days after his loss to Uzcudun.

Like Dempsey, Baer was known to love the company of beautiful women. Hoffman preferred Baer train at Lake Tahoe where the fighter agreed that Hoffman could lock him into his cabin at night. What Hoffman did not know was Baer would crawl out one of the windows and be driven to Reno for a night on the town. He'd arrive back at the lake just before sunrise and crawl back in through the same window just ahead of Hoffman to start the day of training.

Levinsky and his entourage arrived the first week in June and set up training camp south of Reno at Steamboat Springs. The Chicago fighter was managed by his sister – a firebrand known by the nickname "Leaping Lena."

On June 8, all the fight principals were together at Frankie Neal's Fight Emporium for a card headlined by light-heavyweights Denny Lenhart and Mickey McFarland. Dempsey, who served as the referee for the scheduled 10-rounder, was, of course, the main attraction, but the *Gazette* did note the other celebrities in attendance. "A capacity crowd greeted the fighters and received an added thrill when Governor Balzar, King Levinsky, Max Baer, 'Leaping Lena' Levy, Mayor Roberts and One-Eyed Connolly (a famous boxing gate-crasher) were introduced from ringside by Leonard Sacks."

Fight headquarters for Baer-Levinsky were set up at the old Palace gambling house at the corner of Center Street and Commercial Row and tickets went on sale June 9. Dempsey announced $25,000 worth of reservations had been made and he predicted a crowd of 15,000. Sacks and McKay said Dempsey's predictions were always low and they expected an even greater number of spectators

Dempsey also confirmed that he would be training, dividing his time between the two camps. "Whether the ex-champion will don the heavy mitts and box with either Baer or Levinsky during the training period is not known, but he is going to do roadwork and the daily training grind," the *Reno Evening Gazette* reported on June 9.

Everything, it seemed, was going fine – until the Willows burned down.

On June 14, the Willows, a roadhouse owned by Jim McKay and Bill Graham, burned to the ground just as it was being prepared for a grand reopening. The fire broke out about noon and within an hour, the three-story building was destroyed along with thousands of dollars in gambling equipment, luxurious furnishings and boxing equipment that had been used by Jack Johnson when he trained there in 1910 for his bout with Jim Jeffries. Located on Old Verdi Road, now Mayberry Drive, it was known as Rick's Resort at the time. Graham and McKay changed the name to the Willows when they bought it from Rick Di Bernardi in 1922.

The smoke from the fire was visible from throughout the valley and hundreds of onlookers – including Jack Dempsey – made their way to the site via Old Verdi Road to watch it burn. The *Gazette* reported a large traffic jam at the scene.

The fire did give one Reno resident a chance to meet the ex-champion in a comical way. Jack Horgan was a Reno High School student and had just

A group photo taken prior to the Max Baer-King Levinsky fight on July 4, 1932, include (back row from left) actor Wallace Beery, George Wingfield, Morley Griswold, newspaperman Jim Halley, Norman Biltz, Leonard Sacks, Dempsey, Gov. Fred Balzar, actor Tom Mix; (front row) ring announcer Dan Tobey and Reno Mayor E.E. Roberts. *Neal Cobb Collection*

received his letterman's jacket in a ceremony at the school. "I was puffed up 10 feet tall," he said. "We were all standing around the school when we heard the Willows was on fire so a bunch of us jumped in my car and headed over there. I had about seven guys in my car. Well right after we got there, a guy in a big 16-cylinder Cadillac pulled up and he bumped into my car. I got out of the car and I walked stiff-legged over to that car and was going to pull the door open and there sat Jack Dempsey in the driver's seat. I just said 'Hello, Mr. Dempsey. That's some fire, isn't it?' and went back to my car." He didn't even know I was there. He was absorbed in the fire."

McKay said he had the building insured for $75,000, but even with that amount, he'd be taking a considerable loss.

On June 21, the heavyweight championship belt changed hands when Jack Sharkey outpointed Max Schmelling in 15 rounds at the Madison Square

Garden's Long Island Bowl in New York. It was a controversial decision in which many newspaper reporters and fans felt Schmelling had won. Dempsey, apparently tired of training at the camps of Baer and Levinsky, was reached by newspapermen in Los Angeles. The Associated Press reported on June 23, "Dempsey came to Los Angeles yesterday from Reno where he is engaged in promoting fights and a night club. He spent the evening here at a night club with Lina Basquette, former screen actress and dancer."

As late as June 24, fight promoters were considering who would referee the bout. Unlike Baer-Uzcudun the previous year when Dempsey served as the referee and sole judge, Baer-Levinsky would be different. Dempsey removed himself from consideration as the referee and it was announced the judges would be the governors of California and Nevada – "Sunny Jim" Rolph and "Friendly Fred" Balzar. Among the referees being considered were Dave Miller, Ed Purdy and Phil Collins of Chicago, Lou Magnolia and Slim McClelland. Another was Lt. Jack Kennedy of San Francisco – the same Lt. Jack Kennedy who had been the key defense witness in Dempsey's slacker trial a dozen years earlier. Several others also were under consideration but as the *Reno Evening Gazette* speculated "It is generally believed, however, that at the last minute Dempsey will take over the job, as he did last year."

One June 27, it was announced that George Blake of Los Angeles would be the third man in the ring. Blake had refereed the heavyweight title fight between Max Schmelling and Young Stribling the previous July in Cleveland. A day before the fight, it was announced he'd be the sole judge. That freed up Rolph and Balzar to commiserate with their Hollywood friends, and there were plenty of them in town for the fight. Tom Mix had driven up from Los Angeles the day before. Douglas Fairbanks and Mary Pickford were in town as were Douglas Fairbanks Jr., and Joan Crawford. Charlie Chaplin, Buster Keaton, Wallace Beery and Hoot Gibson also made the trip. It was also announced that Dempsey was at Lake Tahoe and would be returning to Reno on the morning of the fight.

In one photo taken inside the ring prior to the fight, Dempsey stood in a group that included Mix and Beery, Balzar, Lt. Gov. Morley Griswold, Reno Mayor E. E. Roberts and even George Wingfield. While Wingfield was well known as political force – not to mention the man behind many of McKay and Graham's ventures – he usually kept himself out of the spotlight.

The crowd was estimated to be about 10,000, far fewer than the Baer-Uzcudun bout of the year before when Uzcudun's fellow Basques accounted for a goodly portion of the 18,000 in attendance. Baer, much more serious and better conditioned than he had been in his loss to Uzcudun, won the

20-round fight by decision. That night, Baer, his manager Ancil Hoffman and Dempsey celebrated. "Ancil was convinced his boy had a chance to gain the title," Dempsey said. Two years later, Baer pounded Primo Carnera at Madison Square Garden to do just that. Dempsey helped Baer schedule his vaudeville dates and formed a partnership with Ancil Hoffman that would last for years.

A few weeks after the Baer-Levinsky fight, Dempsey left Reno again for California. Few knew then, his days as a Reno resident were coming to an end.

19

A Surprise Wedding in Elko

In the early-morning hours of July 18, 1933, a young couple registered at the Mayer Hotel in Elko under the names Mike Costello and Jane Gray. They could have registered as Franklin and Eleanor Roosevelt and received no less attention. Within minutes, news spread through Elko like wildfire that Jack Dempsey was in town and, oh by the way, his fiancé, Hannah Williams, the Broadway actress, was with him. As the Elko Daily Free Press reported "... Dempsey is so well known through this section of the state, having lived in Wells at one time, that it was but a short time that news of his arrival spread."

One of those who recognized Dempsey immediately was Elko police officer W. W. Cook, who had known Dempsey for 20 years. After shaking hands with the champion, Cook asked if they intended to be married. Dempsey said they were on their way to western Nevada and would be married that night, either in Reno or at the Cal-Neva at Lake Tahoe. Cook offered an alternative. "Why not give Elko a break and be married here?" he asked. "We have had no celebrities here since President Hoover spoke here last November." The couple agreed and Cook went quickly to the Elko County courthouse to make arrangements for the license.

Dempsey and Williams were accompanied by Maurice Cain and Mike Cantwell, who were two of Max Baer's trainers. The group had arrived by car from Salt Lake City that morning. No doubt, Dempsey had been in Salt Lake to introduce his fiancé to his mother, Celia. Their engagement had been announced several weeks earlier and their relationship had been well-publicized for several months.

Dempsey had been divorced from Estelle Taylor for nearly two years, while Hannah had divorced Roger Wolfe Kahn on April 4, 1933 in Reno. While they had known each other casually in the past, it was after Williams moved to Reno to establish residency for her divorce that their relationship blossomed into a romance. They were introduced at a luncheon in Reno. When her divorce was finalized, she left immediately for New York and joined Dempsey there.

At 9:30 a.m., Dempsey, Hannah and the two boxing trainers were gathered in the commissioners' room of the Elko County Court House in front of Justice of the Peace J. A. McFarlane, or Alvin, as the Elko folks called him. Their marriage certificate, file No. 54574, was prepared. They both listed their residence as Washoe County, Nevada. Cantwell, a trainer for heavyweight Max Baer, and Cain, listed as "a business representative" for Dempsey, were noted as the witnesses. While it was supposed to be a private ceremony, several newspaper reporters were allowed inside and details of the couple's vows were reported that afternoon in the *Free Press* and on the national wires:

> "I ... take you to have and to hold from this day forward, for richer for poorer, in sickness and in health until death do us part."
>
> In presenting his bride with a beautiful diamond wedding ring, the ex-champion said: "With this ring I thee wed and pledge unto thee my fidelity."
>
> There was no mention of the word "obey" in the services.

Upon leaving the courthouse, the newlyweds discovered several hundred Elko citizens waiting for them, including a photographer for the *Free Press*. Initially, they objected to having their photo taken, saying that they had been traveling all night and neither was dressed for the occasion. Dempsey was wearing a blue suit and two-toned dress shoes, while Hannah was wearing "a traveling ensemble." The couple relented, however, and said they'd "give the small newspaperman a break."

The Elko crowd gave the newlyweds a rousing sendoff, including tying "a great number of cans" to the back of Dempsey's car while the ceremony was taking place. Long after the Dempseys left Elko bound for a honeymoon at Lake Tahoe, Elko was still abuzz with activity. As news of the wedding spread, newspapers from around the country called and wired the *Free Press* office for photos and details. In an editorial the following day, the *Free Press*

Dempsey and his third wife, Hannah Williams, enjoy a celebratory dinner on their honeymoon at Nick Abelman's Stateline Club at Lake Tahoe. *Bill Pettite Collection*

tried to put the story into historical perspective. "The last big story which brought Elko before the nation was made by Ex-President Herbert Hoover, who closed his campaign for the presidency in this city."

The editorial writer seemed far more impressed with Dempsey than with Hoover – or with Dempsey's new wife. "Jack Dempsey has been an idol of many Americans for many years. ... One thing, which must be said, is he always gave the public a run for their money. Another reason he is liked by the average man of the street is that he is friendly; he is a showman, but with his showmanship he shows that he has not lost the common touch, which makes it possible for him to move with the most lowly. His bride, Hannah Williams, seemed to be the typical stage type; she was very pleasant, however, and made a good impression on Elko people who met her before the marriage ceremony."

The *Free Press* also used the opportunity to poke a little fun at Reno, the nation's divorce capital, which rarely had competition from other cities in the state when it came to the national spotlight. "We know of course that Reno would have liked to have had the publicity – it would have been great stuff for 'the biggest little city in the world,' but this was one time that Elko stole Reno's thunder. Better luck next time Reno."

In marrying Hannah, Dempsey was eager not to repeat the mistake that had led to his divorce with Estelle, who had blamed him for the sour turn in her acting career. "I laid it on the line with Hannah," Dempsey said in his autobiography. "I wanted a home and kids, not a life hanging around a stage door or a movie lot, waiting for her to get off work. That's just what she wanted, too, Hannah said." In an interview with reporters in Reno on the day of their wedding, Hannah was quoted as saying "I am all through with the stage. I am going to concentrate on being a good wife to Jack."

The Dempseys honeymooned around Reno and Lake Tahoe for more than a week, including enjoying a dinner with a large group of friends at Nick Abelman's Stateline Country Club on Tahoe's south shore. (The site of present-day Harrah's Lake Tahoe.)

They also went to Los Angeles and visited with friends in Hollywood before returning to Nevada at the end of July. This time, it was to Las Vegas, where Jack Dempsey mixed a little business with pleasure. The *Las Vegas Evening Review-Journal* carried a banner headline on its sports section on July 29 reading "Dempsey coming to Vegas" and followed it two days later with another banner headline: "Dempsey here for card tonight."

> Jack Dempsey, champ of champs, makes his first formal bow to the fistic fans of Las Vegas this evening in the American Legion stadium on South Third Street, when he stages his monster athletic carnival, which will be featured by Dempsey's "cheerful little earful", the former Hannah Williams, now Mrs. William Harrison Dempsey.

Dempsey's "monster athletic carnival" included boxing matches and wrestling. The main event was a six-round heavyweight boxing match between Las Vegan "Poison" Smith and Harry Newman, a "giant heavyweight" from Salt Lake City who Dempsey was touting as "a better prospect right now than was Max Baer when the latter was Newman's age."

As it turned out, Poison Smith thrilled his hometown crowd by pummeling Newman so badly in the third and fourth rounds that Newman's second threw in the towel prior to the start of the fifth round. It was a popular outcome with the fans who packed the arena. "… The walls of the stadium echoed to an ovation that nearly out-sounded the greeting given the old Man Mauler – Jack Dempsey – himself," the *Review-Journal* reported.

John Cahlan, the *Review-Journal* reporter who had met Dempsey at the

Baer-Uzcundun fight in Reno in 1931, said Dempsey was impressed with Smith and another fighter on the card. He related the story to the University of Nevada Oral History Program in 1970.

> … On the fight card were two local fighters by the name of "Poison" Smith and Joe Morales. Dempsey was quite interested in the two of them and thought they were pretty good fighters, so he asked me if I could get them under contract for him, and I told him I thought I could; I'd see what I could do.
>
> So I got the two of them under contract to Dempsey. And he ordered the kids down to southern California for further training. Poison Smith was a great big Negro boy about six feet two and had very long arms and a very small head, and when he got his arms up in front of his head, nobody could get through to him. He was a very good fighter but didn't have any killer instinct. He went down to Los Angeles and went under the wing down there of one of the promoters in that area and got several fights and did very well until he ran up against "Hank" Hankensen, who at that time was quite a Swedish fighter down around the Los Angeles area. And Poison had Hankensen on the deck two or three times during the first couple of rounds, but didn't move in to knock him out, and finally, Hankensen knocked Smith out. And the Dempsey representative under whose wing Smith was fighting, said that he just didn't have it, and was shipping him back. So Poison Smith came back here, and the last I heard of him, he was driving a garbage truck in the city of Las Vegas, but he's still around. Here was a kid that had a real good chance, and with Dempsey's backing probably could've gone somewhere if he had only had the heart to fight.
>
> Joe Morales was quite a different type kid. He was a little Mexican boy, weighed around a hundred and twenty-five or a hundred and thirty pounds, and a real good fighter. The fella in Los Angeles who trained him said that they could've made him the featherweight titleholder — featherweight champion — within two or

three years. He was that good. But unfortunately, the World War broke out, and he enlisted in the Army, and Joe now is over on Anzio Beach under a cross. He was killed in the invasion of Anzio, during World War II.

After the Las Vegas event, Dempsey told reporters he would likely be back with another show in the fall. However, that would not be the case. His time as a Nevada resident was over.

20
World War II Bond Salesman

By the mid 1930s, George Wingfield's banks had collapsed and Bill Graham and James McKay were on trial for federal mail fraud charges. (After two mistrials, they were convicted and sent to federal prison for 10 years, despite Dempsey's testimony on their behalf.) Dempsey, now married to Hannah Williams, mainly split his time between New York and Los Angeles with few, if any, visits to Reno publicized. Still, an event in Reno did briefly bring Dempsey some more negative national attention.

In July of 1934, Washoe County District Attorney Melvin Jepson filed charges of perjury against McKay, who was in New York on trial for the federal mail fraud charges. The charges stemmed from McKay's testimony in Dempsey's 1931 divorce action against Estelle Taylor. McKay had been Dempsey's residency witness and claimed at the divorce trial that he had seen Dempsey in Nevada every day from April 11, 1931 to August 31, 1931. In his federal trial, McKay testified that he had been undergoing treatment in a Vallejo, California hospital in July of 1931. Jepson claimed McKay was in Reno at the time, and engaged in bunco operations.

Jepson's action had some unexpected consequences as newspapers across the country wrote their stories from the angle that the case against McKay might mean Dempsey's divorce from Estelle Taylor was in jeopardy. The *Nevada State Journal's* banner headline read "M'Kay accused of perjury in Dempsey divorce case" with a subhead that read "Ex-fighter's divorce might be attacked." Dempsey himself was enraged. "It's a joke," he was quoted as saying in a United Press article on July 29, 1934. "Why, everyone in Nevada

Jack Dempsey served as a commander in the U.S. Coast Guard during World War II. He led numerous bond drives, including one that stopped in Reno.
Colleen Rosencrantz Collection

knows I was out there six months. Plenty more than the six weeks the law requires. I don't know what this fellow Jepson is trying to do, but doesn't the law mean anything in Nevada anymore?"

The next day, the *Journal*, apparently forgetting its own inflammatory headline of a few days earlier, carried a story that contained the following lead paragraph under the headline "District Attorney Denies Dempsey Divorce Attack."

> Commenting on the articles that have appeared in eastern papers, regarding a possible attack on the legality of the divorce obtained by Jack Dempsey in Reno some time ago, District Attorney Melvin E. Jepson said yesterday that he had never considered or intimated that the divorce was anything but valid.
>
> He said he knew personally that Dempsey had been in the state considerably more than the required time to establish residence, and he was concerned only with the evidence offered by James McKay at the time the divorce was granted here, and with conflicting testimony offered elsewhere.

Jepson went on to say that Dempsey "purchased a home here in Reno and he now may be a bonafide resident of this state for all I know."

A few days later, Hannah gave birth to the Dempseys' first child, a daughter, Joan, at Polytechnic Hospital in New York. The Journal ran the United Press wire story under the headline "Next One Will Be A Boy, Says Dempsey."

At any rate, Dempsey was content to be living in New York. He had opened a restaurant on Broadway and spent much of his time there, though there were frequent trips across country to Hollywood and to Salt Lake to visit his mother. If he came to Reno anytime in the next 10 years, it wasn't a publicized visit.

Another daughter, Barbara, was born in 1937. Shortly thereafter, Hannah decided she wanted to go back into show business and the marriage began falling apart. They had several long separations and the marriage eventually ended in July of 1943 in what Dempsey called "a sensational divorce action." It came at a hectic time in his life.

After the Japanese bombed Pearl Harbor, 46-year-old Jack Dempsey volunteered for service in the Army. He was turned down because of his age. Still haunted by the slacker charges of 21 years earlier, Dempsey was determined to serve his country and he went up the political ladder, by some accounts all the way to Franklin Roosevelt in the White House. He initially joined the New York State National Guard and was commissioned as a first lieutenant. He resigned that commission in order to accept one in the U.S. Coast Guard Reserve.

Lt. Jack Dempsey, who was later promoted to lieutenant commander and commander, reported for active duty on June 12, 1942 at the Coast Guard Training Station at Manhattan Beach in Brooklyn, taking on the duties of "Director of Physical Education." His other duties were to make personal appearances at military camps, hospitals, fights and War Bond drives.

It was the latter that led him to back to Reno on July 3, 1944. On July 2, the *Nevada State Journal* ran a photo of Dempsey with the following caption:

> Jack Dempsey, who once made his home in Reno while promoting the Baer-Uzcudun and Baer-Levinsky 20-rounders a decade ago, also while he launched a lengthy comeback tour in the early '30s, will be here Monday on his bond-selling campaign. Dempsey has been doing a great job directing the Coast Guard's physical training program.

Dempsey's itinerary called for him to arrive in Reno at 8:50 a.m. and depart by plane for San Francisco at 1:50 p.m. He was to meet with his old pal William Woodburn of Washoe County's war bond committee. Woodburn was among the business leaders who had backed the ill-fated effort to arrange a Dempsey-Carnera bout in Reno in the summer of 1932. The goal of Dempsey's war bond visit was to raise in the neighborhood of $500,000 for the war effort. Organizers were counting on Dempsey's popularity, as the *Journal* explained in a separate story:

> The former heavyweight champion, who is no stranger to Reno, and in fact claims this as his home, will be at a bond booth on Virginia Street for a couple of hours during the morning where he will autograph anything but checks in exchange for bond purchases. He will be the honored guest at luncheon at the Riverside hotel at noon where bonds will flow freely and he may have some time to visit some of the clubs.

Dempsey's visit was a success, raising $456,000 in bond sales for the war effort. The luncheon included Dempsey and Warrant Officer John Deer of the Coast Guard, Woodburn and "about 30 bond workers." Ernest Brooks, chairman of the Washoe bond effort, presided over the event and introduced Woodburn, a Reno lawyer, as "Washoe County's top salesman." Woodburn, in turn, introduced Dempsey, who told the audience that selling war bonds was becoming more difficult, but the money was still desperately needed. "We must meet our obligations to the men who are overseas," he said.

Newspapers reports also mentioned Dempsey's "east coast" pronunciation of Nevada, with an elongated "ah" in the second syllable. It's perhaps the only time a Nevada crowd cheered someone who mispronounced the name of the state. Jack Dempsey had earned an exception.

Dempsey quickly departed Reno after the luncheon for his flight to San Francisco.

Later in 1944, he was assigned to the transport USS Wakefield and in 1945, he was on the attack transport USS Arthur Middleton for the invasion of Okinawa. He was 49 years old and a national icon. As troops loaded into small boats for the beach landing, a line officer told Dempsey, "You stay here with me, Jack. We can't afford to lose you." Dempsey replied, "Sir, I trained these boys and they look up to me. I go where they go."

Dempsey was awarded a Legion of Merit for his service. He remained on active duty with the Coast Guard through September 1945 and received an honorable discharge from the Coast Guard Reserve in 1952.

With World War II over, the country returned to a more normal state and the travel restrictions of the war years were lifted. Americans were free to travel at will and nobody loved to travel more than the once-again single Jack Dempsey. He had friends around the country, including many in Nevada.

Jack Dempsey poses with Freck Lydon in Tonopah during the Nevada city's 50th anniversary celebration. Dempsey was the guest of honor and honorary mayor of the city. *Central Nevada Museum*

21

Honorary Mayor of Tonopah

In January of 1950 – 31 years after he'd won the world heavyweight championship and 24 years after he'd lost it – Jack Dempsey was voted the greatest fighter of the first half of the 20th century in an Associated Press poll of sports writers and broadcasters. Dempsey received 251 votes, finishing well ahead of second-place Joe Louis, who received 104.

That same year, Tonopah was celebrating its 50th birthday and the committee, which included Johnny Sudenberg's old sparring partner, Freck Lydon, invited Dempsey to the festivities. Much to the delight of central Nevada, he said yes. On May 14, 1950, the *Goldfield News and Beatty Bulletin* put out an extra edition with a headline the size generally reserved for declarations of war.

Extra!
DEMPSEY
COMING
To Tonopah's 50th Anniversary

Ex-Heavyweight Champion Jack Dempsey, the Manassa Mauler himself, is coming back to the scenes of his earliest encounters. The most popular champion the world has ever known confirmed yesterday that he will be in Tonopah next Saturday, May 20, to officiate the boxing bouts that night and will probably remain for the climactic program the following day.

The *Tonopah Times-Bonanza* reported in its May 19, 1950 edition that Dempsey was making the trip from Santa Monica, Calif., and would arrive in Tonopah the following afternoon. "Upon his arrival here, Dempsey will be made both honorary mayor and chairman of the anniversary committee. A buffet lunch and cocktail party in his honor will be held at the 20-30 clubhouse at five in the afternoon, at which time he will be presented with a belt buckle suitably engraved and designed with a picture of Jim Butler's famous burro."

It was Butler who discovered the vein of silver on May 19, 1900 that led to Tonopah's existence.

Dempsey stopped in Las Vegas on his way to Tonopah and joined company with *Las Vegas Sun* owner Hank Greenspun and Wilbur Clark, who owned the Desert Inn casino. Dempsey and Greenspun had a close friendship. A year earlier, Greenspun had been indicted by the U.S. government for violating the Neutrality Act by taking arms and airplanes to Palestine as Israel was struggling to be born. Dempsey, in Los Angeles at the time, read of Greenspun's indictment and immediately went to Las Vegas, telling Greenspun to pack a bag because they were headed for Washington. As Greenspun later recalled: "We spent an entire week in Washington calling on top governmental leaders who were anxious to do Jack a favor, but we kept running into stone walls and governmental red tape. ... Dempsey argued and fought, threatening to go to the president, and I never will forget his final shot at (Attorney General Brian) McGrath who was a close friend of his. Jack said, 'History will record Hank Greenspun as a hero, and no two-bit politician is going to make a bum out of him.'"

Despite Dempsey's best efforts, Greenspun was convicted. He was fined $10,000. Still, Greenspun never forgot the effort by Dempsey. "I am particularly indebted to The Champ, for he was one of the few who brought me encouragement when the world looked dark indeed." (Greenspun was later pardoned by President John F. Kennedy.)

In Tonopah, Dempsey, Greenspun and Clark checked into a room at the Mizpah Hotel and waited for a call from the welcoming committee. He was scheduled to give a speech at the reception hosted by Tonopah's 20-30 Club. When the call came, they walked to the lobby, three abreast with Dempsey and Clark flanking Greenspun. That's when one of the women from the committee rushed forward, straight to Greenspun, grasped his hand and said: "Oh, Mr. Dempsey. I'm so very thrilled! I've waited years for this great honor!"

Dempsey later recalled: "Wilbur and I were almost doubled up with laughter, but the woman ignored us. Hank, thinking fast, did the only thing he could do under the circumstances: He leaned forward and kissed her noisily on the cheek. The woman turned crimson and breathed 'Wait'll the girls hear bout this! Oh, Mr. Dempsey.' That night, the dinner was a huge success, but I couldn't help wondering what the lady's reaction had been when I was introduced and gave my speech."

Thousands of people poured into Tonopah for the celebration, including Nevada Gov. Vail Pittman and powerful U.S. Sen. Pat McCarran, among others, but Dempsey was clearly the star of the event.

Dempsey's old Nevada business partners, Bill Graham and Jim McKay, made the trip down from Reno. McKay, a new father, brought his whole family, including two-month old son James Jr., who became the subject of a story in the Goldfield paper.

> If former heavyweight champion Jack Dempsey has his way, two-month old James C. McKay Jr., son of Mr. and Mrs. Jim McKay of Reno, will grow up to be a fighter.
>
> Dempsey's offer to "sign as trainer" for the infant was made during Saturday's reception in the 20-30 Club, with beauteous Mrs. McKay protesting that her son is much too young to consider such a possibility.
>
> "Why, he only weighs 12 pounds," she cried in simulated horror.
>
> To which Dempsey replied, "I believe in starting them young."
>
> The proud father, a former Goldfield resident, wasn't so squeamish, however, and said he'd give Dempsey's proposal serious consideration.

During the luncheon, Dempsey received a surprise gift from a local woman, Mrs. Alexander LeBarthe of Goldfield, who presented the champion with a bottle of 138-year-old Napolean cognac. She explained that her late first husband, Marius Durand, had been an old friend of Dempsey's and had promoted one of his earliest fights in Cripple Creek, Colorado when Dempsey was a teenager. Durand later founded the Mozart Club in Goldfield. Mrs. LeBarthe said she'd been saving the bottle of cognac since Durand's death for "a special occasion" and she reckoned there was none - better than this. Her present husband, Alexander LeBarthe, joked about the incident in a 1993 oral history. "Mr. Durand had some real expensive liquor.

He bought a case of Napolean Cognac that was 137 years old. It cost him quite a bit of money. He gave bottles to some of his best friends, but he kept one bottle. In 1950, Mr. Durand was dead, but Mrs. Durand presented this bottle of cognac to Jack Dempsey up there in Tonopah. I said to her, 'What did you give it to Jack Dempsey for? Why don't you give it to me?'"

In the 1940s, Dempsey had also intervened – at the request of Marius Durand – to help prolong the life of the Tonopah & Goldfield Railroad. As transportation and roads improved, the need to transport people, mail and freight on the rails diminished. Busses had replaced passenger cars and gasoline-powered trucks were taking much of the mail and freight. The Tonopah & Goldfield had the mail contract, but there was talk that it was about to end, which would mean doom for the railroad. *Old West* magazine, in its Fall 1979 edition, described Dempsey's role in saving the railroad:

> There's a heart throb in the story of how the fatal day for the T&G was postponed. At the Mozart Club in Goldfield some years ago a little old Frenchman who helped to save the road, temporarily at least, often told this story. (About 1943), Mr. Peck, the superintendent, had said the bus lines were going to start passenger service and it meant ruin for the railroad if the mail and freighting service was lost. Little monsieur Durand sat down and wrote a letter to his old friend, Jack Dempsey.
>
> "Jack will come here to see us soon. Years ago was I not the first man to promote him in Cripple Creek, Colorado in 1913? Jack and George Copeland, in a preliminary – and Jack won in seven rounds – a knockout! ... We wrote Jack telling him about our trains. We ask him to talk to Monsieur Farley (Postmaster General James Farley, an old friend of Dempsey's) about us.
>
> "Jack sends me a nice letter which sounds just like him. He say he very sorry they are trying to put the old camp on the blink. He also say Jim Farley was a regular fellow and it would not be his wish to see any railroad not running so any community would suffer by not having mail delivered to them, and he would do all he could to help us and the old T&G.
>
> "You see? Other people wrote letters. Jack kept his word, and the little T&G train, she still is here, still

running. That was three years ago – but how long she
will run – who knows?

The railroad finally closed on Oct. 15, 1947. In the end, Dempsey and
the residents of Tonopah and Goldfield couldn't save it, but they did prolong
its life.

The Reno papers took notice of Dempsey's 1950 visit to Tonopah as
well. The *Nevada State Journal* reported: "(The) most famous figure mingling
with the crowds here is Jack Dempsey, one of the greatest heavyweight boxing champions of all time. He's here as honorary chairman of the celebration
and honorary mayor of Tonopah."

Dempsey refereed a boxing card, posed for photographs with dignitaries
including Governor Vail Pittman, and generally spent the time renewing old
friendships. On Sunday, he rode in the parade, just behind Pittman and Lieutenant Governor Cliff Jones. He later took the time to visit with reporters
and recall his early fights in Nevada, especially his battles with Sudenberg in
Tonopah and Goldfield.

"They were two of the toughest fights in my entire career," he told
reporters.

Dempsey also clarified one of the long-held myths about his time in
Nevada: "No, I never worked as a bouncer in a Goldfield saloon, but it was
only because nobody would give me the job. I sure would have taken it in
those days."

Dempsey had clearly won over the reporters as this paragraph in the
Goldfield News illustrates: "The affable Dempsey, who seemed to enjoy re-
calling his early career in this section, said that he will never forget the
wonderful way he was treated by the people here. 'I always liked their way of
doing things, and I still do,' he said."

Jack Dempsey clowns with longtime friend Dick Evans at the Eastside Inn in Reno in 1964. *Evelyn Pace Collection*

22

Fake Vomit, Hot Feet
and the FBI

Throughout the 1950s and '60s Jack Dempsey was a frequent visitor to Nevada. Jack Dempsey's Restaurant on Broadway in New York City had become his base, but Dempsey still possessed the wanderlust of his youth. In addition, his daughters both lived in Los Angeles, so Dempsey was constantly criss-crossing the country to visit them.

He still maintained close friendships in Nevada, including those with Bill Graham and James McKay, who had each received pardons from President Harry Truman after their mail fraud convictions and were back in business in Reno.

And there were many other friends as well. On most occasions, Dempsey's Reno visits included stops at Dick and Ernie's Eastside Inn on East Fourth Street, a popular bar owned by brothers Dick and Ernie Evans. Dick Evans was a world-ranked middleweight boxer who fought from the late 1920s through the mid 1940s. He had attended the Dempsey-Willard fight in 1919 and officially met the champion a few years later as Evans was preparing for a fight with Phil "KO" Kaplan in Madison Square Garden. Dempsey came into his dressing room and wished him luck. A friendship was born. Dick Evans retired from the ring in 1943 and he and his brother opened the Eastside Inn in Reno in 1947.

The bar became, according to longtime Reno sportswriter Ty Cobb, "a Mecca for ex-fighters and ring fans." It's decorations were photographs, posters and news clippings of long-ago bouts. Among the well-known patrons were boxers Archie Moore, Max Baer, Young Corbett III, Fred Apostoli and former light-heavyweight champion Maxie Rosenbloom, a one-time opponent of Dick Evans (Rosenbloom won a 10-round decision in Rochester, N.Y. in 1928). Jack Dempsey was also a regular visitor when he was in town.

Dick Evans, like Dempsey, was a supreme practical joker. He kept a phone on the bar that would squirt water into the face of unsuspecting victims. He also had fake vomit and other tricks at the ready, including books of matches that could be used to give an unaware patron a hot foot. Dempsey, who had once given one of his bodyguards a hot foot to the delight of President Franklin D. Roosevelt, loved and shared Evans sense of humor. The old fighters became close friends. Somewhere along the line, Dempsey gave Evans an old fight bell that Dempsey said was the bell used during his championship-winning bout with Jess Willard in Toledo in 1919. Dick Evans used to ring the bell and introduce customers as they entered the bar in much the same way ring announcers introduced the principals in fights. Today, the bell hangs in Jake's Place, a Reno restaurant owned by boxing enthusiast John Pinocchio. It was loaned to Pinocchio by Evelyn Pace of Reno, whose father was Dick Evans.

Evans' grandson, Jim Pace, has a large photo of Dempsey posing with the Evans brothers, Pace's uncle Max Evans, Max Baer and Harold Smith, who owned Harolds Club and frequented the Eastside Inn. The photo hangs on Pace's classroom wall at Reno High School where he is a social studies teacher.

When in Reno in the early 1950s, Dempsey usually stayed at the Golden Hotel, 219 North Center Street, which featured a huge casino and entertainment that included Cab Calloway, Tennessee Ernie Ford, Liberace and other top acts of the day. He was there in June of 1953 to promote Acme-Bulldog Beer to local distributors and entertained a luncheon crowd with tales of his earlier days in Nevada.

As he often did, Dempsey recalled his bouts with Johnny Sudenberg in 1915 as among the toughest in his career. He told of his wheelbarrow ride in Goldfield, of the robbery in the Cobweb bar that left he and Sudenberg broke and their subsequent handcar trip to Mina Junction where they fought in a bar and split $3 for their efforts.

He also told a few whoppers, including that he had met Tex Rickard in Goldfield and had traveled via the rods to Reno in 1910 to watch the Johnson-Jeffries bout. Both were untrue, but entertained the crowd nonetheless.

Dempsey also took time to pose for a photo with Golden Hotel employees Cliff Schellin, Howard King and Baby Moe Macias, all former boxers who worked at the hotel.

Accompanied by his daughters Barbara and Joan, Dempsey stayed at the Golden through the weekend and then they all traveled with Bill Graham to Ogden, Utah for the Maxim-Moore light-heavyweight title fight.

In August of 1953, the 58-year-old Dempsey was again in Reno and took a room at the Golden Hotel. While this trip escaped the notice of the Reno media, it did not escape the notice of the Federal Bureau of Investigation, which, under the direction of J. Edgar Hoover, liked to keep tabs on numerous Americans. A memo from the Salt Lake City office of the FBI, dated August 19, 1953, detailed information from a confidential informant on Dempsey's visit. The names of the informant and several others were blacked out on the memo, which was made public in 1998. It read:

> For the information of the Bureau, (name redacted) has advised that when Jack Dempsey recently visited Reno, Nevada, he stayed at the Golden Hotel. As the Bureau is aware, the hotel has been owned for a number of years by (name redacted), who according to the informant, and according to common knowledge is an old time friend of Dempsey. The informant also is an old time friend of Dempsey.
>
> The informant claims that while Dempsey was staying at the hotel, (name redacted), who is (title redacted) of the establishment, made a chorus girl available for Dempsey's pleasure. According to the informant, Dempsey paid her generously. The informant claims that Dempsey himself told the informant that the chorus girl was made available, and since it is not known how general this information is around the hotel, it is requested the informant's identity be protected.

According to gaming historian Dwayne Kling in his book "The Rise of the Biggest Little City," the Golden Hotel was owned by Frank Hofues in 1953. Bill Graham leased and operated the casino inside the hotel. The identity of the informant is unknown except to the FBI. In 1953, Dempsey had numerous old time friends in Reno from his 1931 and 1932 enterprises.

Whether the FBI watched any of Dempsey's other Nevada visits isn't known. He also spent time in Las Vegas, where he was friendly with many of the casino owners. He'd been a guest when Benny Binion opened his Westerner casino in 1947 and was known to spend time around Binion's Horse-shoe Club and other properties in the city, including Wilbur Clark's Desert Inn. Wilbur Clark had once worked as a dealer at Reno's Bank Club, which was owned by Graham and McKay.

In February of 1961, Dempsey made a trip back to Elko County, this one 27 years after his impromptu wedding to Hannah Williams at the Elko County Courthouse. In mid-January of 1961, he had accepted an invitation from the Elko Elks to be the keynote speaker at the civic group's annual Youth Night.

The Elks quickly put together a committee to prepare for the event. It was made up of co-chairmen Frank Harris and Lynn Burns, John "Swede" Flowers and Johnny Gammick, who was named publicity chairman of the event. Tickets went on sale a week later – 250 of them for $2.50 each – and Ernie Hall, exalted ruler of the Elko Elks Lodge, expected them to sell quickly. The dinner and program would be held in the Frontier Room of the Commercial Hotel and arrangements had been made for Little League play-ers, Babe Ruth League players, and the high school football and basketball teams to attend.

A few days before the Elko event, it was announced that Dempsey would stop in Wells to address high school students at a special assembly and then proceed to the Nevada School of Industry for another short talk. It was also announced Dempsey would be traveling with his fourth wife, Deanna, a New York jewelry shop owner he had married in 1958; and Al Wardin, the sports editor of the *Ogden Daily Examiner* in Ogden, Utah.

A frightening moment happened just before the Elko trip. Dempsey and his wife were in Salt Lake City where the champion was scheduled to give a speech. He also used the opportunity to visit his sister, Effie, who was in her 90s. He and Deanna checked into the Hotel Utah, but when they went to bed that night, Deanna was restless and couldn't sleep. Dempsey had no trouble nodding off, but awoke at 3 a.m. to find his wife still wide awake. He grumpily told her to shut the light off. Dempsey recalled the rest of the story in his 1977 autobiography.

> At four o'clock, someone pounded on the door, screaming "Fire!" Anyone with a heart condition would have died there and then. I looked at my wife, who was spooked and white as chalk, and told her to hurry. Within two minutes we were outside and the fire had been put out.

Returning to our room, I threw myself back into bed and fell asleep almost immediately. Then I was reawakened by the press, who wanted to interview me. I struggled up, dressed and made my way downstairs, only to be asked to change to my bathrobe and muss up my hair, since it would look better. By the time I made it downstairs again, I looked as if I had been through not only a fire, but an earthquake and a flood as well.

"Jack, can you tell us what was your toughest fight?"

I sighed and said, "Getting my wife out of the room without her makeup."

The *Elko Daily Free Press* ran the photo of Dempsey sitting in his bathrobe in its Feb. 7 edition, the day of Dempsey's visit.

The great Manassa Mauler received a hero's welcome in Nevada. The Nevada Highway Patrol met his group at the state line in Wendover and escorted it to Wells and then to the Nevada School of Industry, a school for delinquent and needy youths, now known as the Nevada Youth Training Center. He was met there by a welcoming committee from Elko that included Johnny Gammick, Frank Harris, Lynn Burns, Swede Flowers, Ernie Hall and Chris Sheerin, editor of the *Free Press*, who had been a cub reporter at the newspaper in 1933 when Dempsey dropped in for his surprise wedding. Sheerin recalled the meeting in an editorial in the Feb. 7, 1961 edition of the *Free Press*.

Jack will always be remembered as one of the great fighters. We can remember when he was married in Elko. We rushed up to the Scott Studio, picked up a camera and rushed to the court house to get a picture of Dempsey and his new bride. She was not about to have her picture taken as they had driven from Salt Lake City during the night and she felt her hair was slightly askew.

The writer said to Jack, "come on Jack, give a small town newspaperman a break."

Jack turned to his bride and said, "Let's give him a picture, honey.

And they did.

Since then, the writer has always had a soft spot in his heart for Dempsey.

Dempsey's Elko speech was a sellout and he didn't disappoint. After a brief speech, he showed films of some of his more memorable fights, including the "long count" bout with Gene Tunney. He also signed numerous autographs for the youngsters, including signing a copy of his autobiography for a young Richard Gammick, who is today the district attorney of Washoe County in western Nevada.

Shortly after his speech, Dempsey and his entourage were back on the road, driving across Nevada on their way to California.

23

An Interview at
Powning Park

I n a casual conversation with one of his lawyers in Los Angeles in
1964, Jack Dempsey discovered his fourth wife Deanna's 1958 Tijuana
divorce – and their subsequent wedding in the same Mexican city – were
not valid in the United States. In fact, his wife was still technically married
to her previous husband, Bruno Piatelli.

Though they had been together for six years, the Dempseys wanted to
set things straight. As Dempsey recalled in his 1977 autobiography: "Deanna
and I then made plans for her to go to Reno for six weeks to establish residency for divorce. Because we didn't want publicity at this time, she checked
into a local boarding house. ... I stayed away from her for about two weeks
before I went to Reno, almost a madman because of the insecurity I still felt
when it came to wives. We checked into a small Reno hotel within walking
distance of the boarding house."

Famous visitors were commonplace for Reno in the early 1960s.
Between the divorce trade and entertainment venues at the hotel-casinos, the
famous flocked to Reno. They included Marilyn Monroe, Clark Gable,
Montgomery Clift and John Huston – all in town for the filming of "The
Misfits" in 1960. Frank Sinatra and his Rat Pack pals Sammy Davis Jr.,
and Dean Martin were frequent visitors, as were the boys of the Ponderosa
Ranch – Lorne Green, Dan Blocker, Pernell Roberts and Michael Landon.

But a Reno stop by Jack Dempsey was still something special, especially
for an editor for the *Reno Evening Gazette* named Rollan Melton. "When I

was growing up, my father, every day or so, would bring up Jack Dempsey's name," Melton recalled in a 1983 column in the *Reno Gazette-Journal*. "Dad would crouch there in our little house, bob and weave, crashing hooks and uppercuts on an imaginary enemy and say, 'This was Jack's style, son. He was the greatest of our champions.'"

So in October of 1964, when Melton received a tip that Dempsey was in Reno, staying at the Holiday Lodge on South Center Street, he was determined to get an interview. It proved to be much easier than he imagined. Melton called the motel and was connected with Dempsey's room. "Love to visit you, friend," Dempsey said. "You meet me here and we'll take a little walk together." Melton quickly contacted longtime Reno photographer Don Dondero, and they headed for Dempsey's room together.

Details of the visit appeared on the front page of the October 15, 1964 issue of the *Reno Evening Gazette* under the headline "Interview With a Champion: Dempsey Recalls Old Days In Reno."

> By Rollan Melton
> Three men walked toward Powning Park.
> One had a camera. Another had pencil and paper.
> The third was older. His walk was brisk. He was a step ahead of the others. Passersby stared at the older man.
> The trio hiked north on Center Street, turned over to the Washoe Library.
> It was late afternoon and Powning was cool and pleasant. A patch of sun filtered onto a bench east of the Courthouse. "Let's sit over here a spell," the older man said. "The doctor told me to get some sun."
> "YOU'RE JACK"
> A stranger leaped from the bench. "I'll bet you money you're Jack Dempsey." The older man replied, "That's right." He extended the hand that in 1919 pulverized Jess Willard in Toledo.
> The left – that was the one that put Gene Tunney down for 13 seconds in 1927 – clasped the trembling stranger's shoulder.

The stranger's name was Charles Doyle and he whispered to photographer Dondero, "Is that really Jack Dempsey? My wife won't believe me when I tell her I was this close to the champ." Dondero replied, "Go over there and

Jack Dempsey is interviewed by Reno newsman Rollan Melton at Powning Park in downtown Reno in October 1964. *Marilyn Melton Collection*

sit next to him. I'll take your picture and then your wife will believe you." Doyle did as advised and Dondero took the photo. "I'll bet this photo is prized more than any other I've ever taken," Dondero said.

Dondero shot a roll of film and departed from the scene. Doyle remained on the bench to eavesdrop on the interview. Dempsey explained that he was in Reno on his doctor's advice. He'd been hospitalized earlier in the year with a severe case of bronchitis that left him with an enlarged heart. He said upon his release from the hospital in late September, his doctors told him to follow a salt-free diet, do some walking in the fresh air and get some rest. That advice led him back to Reno, he said. True or not, he did not mention Deanna's pending divorce.

The subject of the interview, instead, turned to Dempsey's Nevada memories:

> "It's a nice thing, being out here again. You know, I did a lot of fighting in Nevada? Tonopah, Ely, Goldfield, Reno."
>
> "One of my vivid memories of Reno dates to '31 when I promoted the Max Baer-Paulino Uzcudun fight. Your governor Balzar … what was his first name? … yeah, Fred, said 'Jack, you're going to referee this thing.' I protested, but ended up doing it."
>
> "It went 20 rounds. I gave the decision to the Basque. Baer was sore. Balzar? I guess he was, too."

Melton went on to describe Dempsey's physical appearance. He had gray in his hair and was heavier, at 212 pounds, than his fighting weight of 197. The champion lamented that many of his Reno friends had passed.

> "Most of my old Nevada buddies are dead now. George Wingfield – he'd give you a fight if he thought he was right; and (state) Sen. Noble Getchell – and many others."
>
> "Of course, Bill Graham's still here. Dr. Vinton Muller. Known him a good many years. And his wife, Maisie, too. Wonderful people."

The interview continued and Dempsey weighed in on a wide variety of subjects ranging from the state of the professional boxing ("There isn't anything about professional boxing today that would cause me to recommend it.") to youngsters ("Get an education, you young people.") to politics ("I like President Johnson. He's a nice fellow. Smart, too.) to getting older ("I'm 69 years old, but I feel good. Health … you realize how precious it is when you get on in years.").

When President Lyndon B. Johnson stopped in Reno on October 12, Dempsey and his wife were there to greet him. A photo of them shaking hands appeared in the *Nevada State Journal* the following day.

Melton recalled the tenor of the conversation with Dempsey in a column a decade later and told how he had been nervous meeting Dempsey and expected to be dismissed quickly. "But with the champ, there was no need. He was as comfortable as worn shoes, as playful as a basket of puppies."

The 1964 interview wrapped up with Dempsey saying that he'd be around town for a while longer. "Dee and I have a nice little room over at the motel. The air is nice here. The people are nice." He signed an autograph for Doyle, who had sat through the entire interview. Melton put his notebook away, still in awe of his childhood hero, and walked Dempsey back to his motel.

Dempsey made few public appearances during his time in Reno. The *Journal* reported that he spent much of his time fishing the Truckee River behind the Holiday Lodge or playing golf on Bud Ruppert's nine-hole course. He also fished at Norman Biltz's private lake near Lake Tahoe. His other public appearances were to speak to the local sportswriters and broadcasters group and visit with the University of Nevada football and boxing teams.

He never mentioned his real reason for being in Reno and the papers, apparently, never found out. Deanna Dempsey's divorce hearing was held a few weeks later at the Reno courthouse. According to court transcripts, she had checked into the Holiday Hotel on Sept. 28, 1964 for one night under her previous married name of Deanna Piatelli and then moved into the Elmhurst Guest House on Willow Street in Reno. The house's proprietor, Katherine Kraii, served as the witness to her residency during the divorce hearing, which was held before Judge Thomas Craven in the Second Judicial District Court in Reno.

Deanna's attorney was T. L. Withers of Reno. George Lohse was the attorney for Bruno Piatelli, who did not attend the hearing and who did not contest the divorce. They had been separated since 1952, so the trial was brief with no objections on either side.

On November 30, the Nevada State Journal ran a story with the headline: "Dempsey Ends Month Vacation In Reno Area; Regains Health."

"I've had some great times and made fine friends in Nevada," Dempsey said. "Next time, I won't stay away so long."

The Dempseys returned to their home in New York. They were married officially in a midnight ceremony in the New York City Hall office of Herman Katz to avoid any press coverage.

Dempsey kept his promise and returned to Reno fairly frequently over the next few years. One person who came to know Dempsey well in the 1960s was Reno native William Pettite, a former judge who also worked for Ancil Hoffman, Max Baer's longtime manager. Pettite, who was a neighbor of Hoffman in Fair Oaks, California, was also the nephew of Nick Abelman, the Goldfield and Reno bar owner who had known Dempsey since 1915. Dempsey and Ancil Hoffman had a number of business interests together and Dempsey often flew into Sacramento and would stay with Hoffman in the Sacramento suburb of Fair Oaks. During these visits, he would often ask Pettite to drive him to Reno to visit friends.

"The years I drove Jack to Reno were from 1963 to 1968," Pettite said. "Jack, upon arrival at Ancil's, would call his Reno friends, Bill Graham and Mrs. June Abelman (Nick Abelman's widow). We would often drive to Reno to see them, usually without press or public knowledge.

"Reno was a favorite place for Dempsey and he talked about being neighbors to Graham and Abelman on California Avenue in the 1930s. He called them, along with James McKay and George Wingfield, 'the syndicate.' Ancil, who sometimes rode along, would correct it to 'the committee.' Both talked about the group's meetings at the Spanish Springs Ranch, (first owned by Reno Mayor E. E. Roberts and then by Nick Abelman, who bought it in 1935 and later sold it to George Wingfield). Jack called them 'shake-hand men,' meaning their word was always good."

Often, Pettite would leave Dempsey in Reno and return a week later to pick him up. Dempsey generally stayed with Bill Graham, but would sometimes take a room at the Riverside or another hotel in the downtown area.

Rod Stock, a retired Reno policeman recalled running into Dempsey one morning in the winter of 1965. "I was walking the beat and had just kind of checked out skid row to see if I had any sleepers when I saw this well-dressed guy in an overcoat leaning on the bridge looking down at the Truckee River," Stock said. "I knew right off who it was. I said, 'Hello, Mr. Dempsey.' We talked for a while. He said, 'I get bored at the restaurant.'"

Dempsey's celebrity status certainly hadn't waned in the 1960s. On August 5, 1966, he joined other celebrities, including fellow heavyweight champion Joe Louis, actors John Wayne, Gregory Peck and Anthony Quinn, and television host Ed Sullivan for the opening of Caesars Palace in Las Vegas. They attended the opening of the Circus Maximus Showroom by watching Andy Williams perform.

As the decade of the 1960s came to a close, so did Dempsey's Nevada visits. Most of his old pals were gone. Jim McKay had died in 1962 and Bill Graham passed in late 1965. Abelman and Wingfield had died years before.

In 1970, Bill Pettite held an 85th birthday celebration for Ancil Hoffman at the Mapes Hotel in Reno, a large extravaganza titled "Reno's Golden Days of Boxing." The event was held in the Sky Room of the Mapes and the boxing greats in attendance included former heavyweight champions Jack

Sharkey, James J. Braddock and Jersey Joe Walcott. Two Ton Tony Galento, Willie Pastrano, Fred Apostoli, Jackie Fields and Jimmy McLarnin were also there. Nevada Governor Paul Laxalt and his brother, Robert, attended the event. Reno tavern owner Dick Evans provided classic fight films from his extensive collection for the event. Hoffman, himself, was too ill to attend after coming down with a bout of pneumonia. He was able to receive well-wishes from those in attendance and communicate with a speaker phone.

Dempsey could not attend. He was on business in Scarsdale, N.Y. with his friend Dave Margolis. The pair sent the following telegram, addressed to Pettite:

> DEAR JUDGE
> IT IS WITH DEEP REGRET THAT WE CANNOT BE WITH YOU ON THIS MOST IMPORTANT DAY TO CELEBRATE WITH YOU AND TO PARTICIPATE IN THE GOLDEN DAYS OF BOXING BANQUET AND TO PAY TRIBUTE TO OUR DEAR PAL ANCIL HOFFMAN ON HIS 85TH BIRTHDAY GOD BLESS FOR MANY MORE YEARS WE SALUTE YOU BILL FOR YOUR UNTIRING EFFORTS AND TO CHARLES MAPES FOR HIS DEVOTION AND WE SALUTE ALL OUR DEAR FRIENDS AND PALS WHO WILL BE HONORED ON THIS MEMORABLE OCCASION GOD BLESS ALL OF YOU WITH EVERY GOOD WISH SINCERELY JACK DEMPSEY AND DAVE MARGOLIS.

After 1970, Pettite said communication with Dempsey was primarily by phone as the former champion stayed in or close to New York City. Any contact with Nevadans came when they stopped into his restaurant. Those contacts stopped when it closed in 1975.

That same year, on a newspaper trip to the Big Apple, Reno newsman Rollan Melton said he tried desperately to get to Dempsey for one last interview. Through his media contacts, Melton was able to get Dempsey's home phone number, but "couldn't get past his housekeeper, who shielded him more effectively than any great boxing trainer. 'Mr. Dempsey just isn't up to an interview,' she said. That was it."

Jack Dempsey's Nevada days were behind him.

A portrait of Jack Dempsey in his 80s. *Reno Gazette-Journal File*

24
A Champion Passes

Jack Dempsey died in his New York apartment on May 31, 1983. He was 87 years old and had been in declining health for years, though he tried to never show it to the public. When he was 80, he still rode his bicycle in Central Park and prior to the closing of his restaurant, he always stood to greet visitors despite painfully arthritic hips.

His death made the front page of newspapers around the country, including the *New York Times*, which ran a tribute prepared by its legendary sportswriter Red Smith, who had died a year earlier. The *Los Angeles Times* ran news of Dempsey's death as its lead story beneath a banner headline: "Jack Dempsey Dies at 87" and a subhead "1920s Boxing Champ Remained a U.S. Hero."

Tributes poured in:

"Jack Dempsey was a champion who never lost his title in the hearts of the American people," President Ronald Reagan said.

Jim Murray, the great columnist for the *Los Angeles Times* wrote: "More than a man died with Dempsey. He took an era with him."

In New York, the Friar's Club ran a death notice in the *New York Times* that read: "The Friars regret the passing of their Fellow Friar, Jack Dempsey on May 31, 1983." – Frank Sinatra, Abbot; William B. Williams, Dean.

Boxing historian Bert Sugar, said: "Jack Dempsey was perhaps the man who sculpted the golden age of sports. Before Babe Ruth hit his height, before there even was a Bobby Jones. Sixty years later, he was still the greatest, regardless of what Muhammad Ali says."

In Reno, columnist Ty Cobb, who had sat in the stands and ruined a new pair of jeans by sitting in the boiling pine pitch on the arena seats at the Baer-Uzcudun bout, recounted Dempsey's history in Nevada and remembered fondly a pair of meetings with the champion. "He occasionally, in later years, visited Reno," Cobb wrote in the *Nevada State Journal*. "We had a nostalgic lunch with him, and his daughters Barbara and Joan, at the Golden Hotel here. … At his famous New York City restaurant, the old champion was a genial host to thousands, and was especially gracious to servicemen. Also to anyone from Nevada. During a New York visit with K. D. (Dal) Dalrymple of Reno, who had known Jack in the old days at Ely, we attracted attention by our silver (real silver then) dollars. He was delighted to find Nevadans and treated us to two dinners where he regaled us with many tales of the old times in one of his favorite states, Nevada."

The *Journal* and *Reno Evening Gazette*, at this time sister papers under the same management, ran a tribute to Dempsey as their primary editorial on June 2, 1983, with the headline: "Dempsey epitomized feeling of an American era." The final paragraph read: "So it is good to remember that once men like Jack Dempsey symbolized an excellence toward which all men could strive, if they wished. That once upon a time a man – and by implication mankind – could straddle the universe."

Reno columnist Rollan Melton, himself a hobo kid who made good, remembered Dempsey as a lifelong hero. "When he died, I joined millions who said, 'A part of my own living history is gone.' We retain the memory, though. Nothing is finer than remembering a champion who was a true champion."

Reno boxing writer Steve Sneddon caught up with 80-year-old Dick Evans, a fighter from Dempsey's era who knew the former champion well. Evans, who grew up in Ohio, had been at the 1919 fight when Dempsey flattened Jess Willard for the championship. In later years, when Evans and his brother, Ernie, owned the Eastside Inn tavern in Reno, Dempsey would visit and reminisce about old times. Evans and Sneddon remembered Dempsey by watching the film of Dempsey's second fight with Gene Tunney, the famous "long count" fight. To Evans, it didn't matter that Dempsey had lost. "That Dempsey was great," Evans said with tears streaming down his face. "I cried when he died. I loved Dempsey. He was a hell of a swell guy."

In the *Las Vegas Sun*, publisher Hank Greenspun mourned the death of his friend.

> The champ of champs is dead.
> There will be no more birthdays for Jack Dempsey,
> just anniversaries of his death.

There will be much written and said of this man,
but two qualities of his character will remain eternal.
He was a tiger in the ring and a pussycat as a friend.
A warm, huggable human being.

I cannot write of his death because I rather remember him as he was in life. … Because he represented
much of what Nevada is …

Jack Dempsey's coffin was draped with an American flag at the Frank E.
Campbell Funeral Home on Madison Avenue and 81st Street in New York.
The wake, though open to the public, was attended mostly by family and
close friends. The great champion had outlived most of his contemporaries.
It had been 68 years since his first Nevada fight against Anamas Campbell in
Reno, and 57 years since he lost his heavyweight championship to Tunney on
a rainy day in Philadelphia.

He was laid to rest in a private ceremony at a cemetery in Southampton,
N.Y. The headstone simply read "Dempsey" at the top and "Jack" as the lone
name. William Harrison Dempsey, Harry Dempsey and Kid Blackie were all
names of a bygone era. A pair of boxing gloves were engraved in the headstone as well, along with this epitaph, from his widow, Deanna: "A gentleman
and a gentle man."

Tex Rickard. *Gary Schultz Collection*

25

The Supporting Players

L ike Dempsey, most of those who helped write his Nevada history are gone. Many of them preceded him in death and their stories are left to be told by their children, grandchildren or a handful of history buffs who find Dempsey's story as fascinating today as the rest of the world did when it was being lived.

Here is a brief look at what became of these key players in Jack Dempsey's Nevada story:

Johnny Sudenberg, Dempsey's opponent in his early fights in Goldfield, Tonopah and Ely – plus a Mina saloon – died Feb. 6, 1976 at Hillhaven Convalescent Hospital in Anaheim, Calif. He had suffered from Parkinson's disease in his later years. In 1970, the *Los Angeles Times* featured a story on him in which he talked about Dempsey and the early years in Tonopah. Dempsey, too, was quoted, saying his fights with Sudenberg were among the toughest in his career.

R. E. "Freck" Lydon, who sparred with Johnny Sudenberg and befriended Dempsey in 1915, and who helped bring Dempsey to Tonopah in 1950, died January 18, 1959. Born in Leadville, Colo., Lydon came to Tonopah in its earliest days and was a miner and boxer of considerable reputation. When he became a peace officer in 1936, he was usually able to handle lawbreakers in the tough mining town with his fists.

Nick Abelman, who owned the Cobweb Club in Tonopah when Dempsey and Sudenberg were robbed at gunpoint after their 1915 fight and who lived near Dempsey on California Avenue in Reno years later, died

Dec. 15, 1951. In 1906, he ran the Bon-Ton Club in Goldfield prior to moving to Tonopah in 1913, where he also operated the Tonopah Club, Big Casino, Nevada Club and the Emporium. He was the primary fight promoter in Tonopah for all the years he lived there. After moving to Reno at the urging of George Wingfield, he was involved in many casino ventures. He owned the ornate Ship & Bottle Club, Stateline Country Club and the Waldorf Club. He also operated the Riverside hotel/casino for 15 years. Like Dempsey, Abelman was known as a kind-hearted man who loaned thousands of dollars to friends and the down-and-out, most of which was never repaid.

George Wingfield, who was in Goldfield when Dempsey fought there and ran the banks in Reno when Dempsey returned in 1931, died on Christmas Day in 1959. Often referred to as "the political boss of Nevada," he maintained numerous interests in the Silver State. He lost his fortune and much of his political power when his banks collapsed in 1932. Through mining interests with Noble Getchell, he regained his wealth, but he never regained his political power.

James McKay, who had designs on becoming "the next Rickard" in fight promotions in late 1931, died June 20, 1962 in Reno after a long illness. After his release from prison in 1945 on mail fraud charges, he and business partner Bill Graham returned to Reno and maintained their interest in the Bank Club and Golden Hotel. In 1950, at the urging of U.S. Sen. Pat McCarran of Nevada, he and Graham were pardoned by President Harry S. Truman.

Bill Graham died Nov. 5, 1965 at his home on California Avenue. He remained an avid boxing fan all his life. At the time of his death, he was making plans to travel to Las Vegas for the Floyd Patterson-Cassius Clay fight. Whenever Dempsey was in northern Nevada or Sacramento in the 1950s and early 1960s, he would often visit Graham in Reno or Graham would drive to Sacramento.

Tex Rickard, the one-time Goldfield, Rawhide and Ely saloon owner, died in Jack Dempsey's arms in a Miami, Fla., hospital in January of 1929. Dempsey called Rickard's mother with the news of her son's passing. The funeral was held in Madison Square Garden in New York and thousands passed by Rickard's coffin as it lay in state. Dempsey returned to Miami to promote the Young Stribling/Jack Sharkey fight in Rickard's stead. Dempsey called Rickard "the greatest fight promoter of all time ... and as great a man as I ever met."

Jack "Doc" Kearns, Dempsey's manager when he won the heavyweight championship, died July 7, 1963 in Miami, Fla. After Dempsey dumped him at the insistence of Estelle Taylor, Kearns filed numerous lawsuits against Dempsey and hounded him for years. In 1964, *Sports Illustrated* ran a book excerpt in which Kearns said he had soaked Dempsey's taped hands in plaster of paris before the start of the Willard fight and his "loaded gloves" were the reason for the destruction of Willard that day. Dempsey sued for libel and the case was settled out of court. Part of the settlement was a formal apology printed in the magazine.

Maxine Cates Dempsey, the champion's first wife, died in 1924. According to Dempsey, she died in a fire in an upstairs bedroom of a brothel where she was working as a prostitute in Juarez, Mexico. No independent accounts of her death have ever been found. There have long been rumors in Nevada that she stayed at the Wells brothel for a time, then changed her name, married and lived the rest of her life in Nevada.

Jerry "The Greek" Luvadis, a trainer who worked with Dempsey for many of his fights, including his comeback launched in Reno, died in September of 1938 at Welfare Hospital of New York after a long battle with cancer. During the second Tunney fight, Luvadis was given the task of tasting all of Dempsey's food and drink to make sure it was safe for the champion.

Gene Tunney, The Fighting Marine, died Nov. 7, 1978 in a Greenwich, Conn., hospital at the age of 80. Reached at home in New York, Dempsey was grief-stricken by the news. "I feel like a part of me is gone," he said. When their fighting days were over, Dempsey and Tunney had become great friends with a sincere mutual respect. In September 1952, Tunney penned a story for Look Magazine in which he said: "Jack Dempsey, I'm convinced, was our greatest heavyweight champion. In his prime, when he knocked out Jess Willard to win the title in 1919, he would have taken the four leading heavyweights of today – Jersey Joe Walcott, Rocky Marciano, Harry (Kid) Matthews and Ezzard Charles – and flattened them all in one night." Dempsey, when asked, always said Tunney was the greatest heavyweight. "He beat Jack Dempsey twice, didn't he?"

Paul Beeler, the knockdown timekeeper in the infamous Dempsey-Tunney "Long Count" fight in Chicago, died May 3, 1970 at his home in Sparks. Beeler spent many years as a scout for the Chicago White Sox. His career, however, was as a railroad shipping and receiving clerk. He lived in Sacramento for 15 years before moving to Sparks in the late 1960s.

Estelle Taylor, Dempsey's second wife whom he came to Reno to divorce in 1931, died of cancer on April 15, 1958, never having achieved the stardom she so desperately sought. *The New York Times* story about her death said "Estelle Taylor won stardom only in her real-life role as Mrs. Dempsey. In the movies, she was a supporting player. She married Broadway producer Paul Small in 1943. They were divorced two years later.

Max Baer, the Livermore butcher boy, died of a heart attack Nov. 21, 1959 in Hollywood, Calif. Baer had recovered from his loss to Paulino Uzcudun in Reno in 1931 and, under the management of Ancil Hoffman, won his next 14 fights, including an 11th round knockout of Primo Carnera on June 14, 1934 for the heavyweight championship. He lost it the following year to James J. Braddock (Cinderella Man). Pallbearers at Baer's funeral in Sacramento included Jack Dempsey and Joe Louis. Max Baer Jr., said his father and Dempsey were more like brothers than friends.

Paulino Uzcudun, the Basque Woodchopper, who beat Baer under the hot Fourth of July sun in Reno in 1931, died July 6, 1985 in Torrelaguna, Spain. He was 86. In 1932, he won the European heavyweight title for the second time when he defeated Pierre Charles of France. His final fight was in 1935 when, lured out of retirement, he was knocked out by Joe Louis. It was the first and only time he had been knocked out in his career.

Leonard Sacks, Dempsey's business manager when he moved to Reno in 1931, died December 29, 1968 at a Sacramento convalescent home after a long illness. The news of his death, as reported in the Sacramento Bee, identified him as a man who "once managed Jack Dempsey."

Fred Balzar, the Nevada governor during Dempsey's residence in Nevada, died March 24, 1934 at the Governor's Mansion in Carson City after a long illness. In addition to Dempsey, "Friendly Fred", as Balzar was known, had numerous high profile friends. Among them was Will Rogers, who died five months later in an Alaska plane crash. Balzar's friendship with Dempsey is mentioned in the book "Nevada's Governors" by Myrtle Myles. It includes a photo of Balzar and Dempsey "sparring" while on a fishing excursion at Pyramid Lake.

Ancil Hoffman, Max Baer's manager and Dempsey's longtime business partner, died in his sleep on January 7, 1976 at his home in Fair Oaks, California. He was 91 years old. In addition to his work as a boxing manager, Hoffman was a businessman and civic leader in the Sacramento area. When he died, he left most of his large estate to Sacramento County. Ancil Hoffman Park and Ancil Hoffman Golf Club are named in his honor. His wife, Maudie, who died in 1986, was raised in Virginia City.

Imey Garfinkle, who ran the Chestnut Street Arena where Dempsey trained for his 1931 comeback, died Nov. 16, 1967 in Reno. A light heavyweight boxer in his day, he had arrived in Reno in 1924 for a bout with Mickey Wallace and returned in 1926 to make it his permanent residence. His final fight was against Reno light heavyweight Tony Poloni. After retiring from the ring, he managed fighters and ran the Chestnut Street Arena.

Lina Basquette, the silent film star who lived with Dempsey in Reno in 1932, died in September 1994 after a long and fascinating life. After she and Dempsey split up, she attempted suicide in Los Angeles and newspaper reports indicated she left a note to Dempsey that read, "I love only you. I couldn't help it. I can't go on without you." Less than a week later, she married Teddy Hayes, her former husband and Dempsey's former trainer. In her life, she married nine times, including three times to Hayes. One of her great admirers in the 1930s was Adolph Hitler and she traveled to Europe to meet him. Later in life, she became a prolific dog breeder and dog handler.

Noble Getchell, the long-time Nevada State Senator and Dempsey's mining partner, died February 10, 1960. For more than 40 years, he was a key player in Nevada Republican politics, but it was his mining ventures that gained him wealth. Much like Tex Rickard, Getchell spent time in the Klondike before making his way to Nevada in 1920. Getchell's greatest mining success came in the late 1930s with the Getchell Mine in Humboldt County, which became the world's second largest gold producer and later became a producer of tungsten ore. The library at the University of Nevada, Reno, completed in 1961, was named in his honor.

Henry O. "Tex" Hall, the Reno gambler who partnered with Dempsey, Getchell and McKay in the mines in Midas, died of a heart attack on June 12, 1936 in Reno. Born Henry Orlando Hall in Texas, he came to Nevada during the boom in Tonopah in 1902 and later moved to Ely where he managed the Northern Hotel. He moved to Reno in 1920 and soon became associated with Graham and McKay. In April of 1935, he was found guilty by a federal jury in San Francisco of conspiring to harbor the notorious bank robber George "Baby Face" Nelson. He was sentenced to one year and a day in federal prison.

Hannah Williams, Dempsey's third wife, died in Hollywood on January 11, 1973. After her divorce from Dempscy in 1943, she married actor Thomas J. Monaghan in 1950, but that marriage also ended in divorce. In March of 1953, she was burned in a hotel fire and Dempsey brought her to New York to recover at his apartment. She left shortly thereafter and returned to Hollywood. Like Estelle Taylor, her acting career never took off as she had hoped.

Hank Greenspun, the Las Vegas newspaperman and close Dempsey friend, died of cancer on July 22, 1989. As publisher of the *Las Vegas Sun*, he fought many battles, including attacks on U.S. Senators Joe McCarthy and Pat McCarran during the era of McCarthyism. The chapter on his conviction for supplying arms to Israel ended when he received a pardon from President John F. Kennedy in 1961.

Wilbur Clark, the owner of the Desert Inn in Las Vegas who accompanied Dempsey and Hank Greenspun to Tonopah in 1950, died August 27, 1965 in La Jolla, California. A native of Keyesport, Illinois, Clark made his way west before finishing high school. He worked as a bellboy at a hotel in San Diego then learned to gamble and deal cards on the gambling ship Rex, which was anchored off Santa Monica. He then made his way to Reno for a time and worked as a dealer at the Bank Club owned by McKay and Graham. He eventually returned to San Diego and then made his way to Las Vegas where he opened the El Rancho. His next venture was the Desert Inn, but had to sell 75 percent interest in it to raise money for its completion. Moe Dalitz, who was associated with the Cleveland mob, was the majority owner, but Clark remained the public face of the Desert Inn.

June Pettite Abelman, Nick Abelman's widow who remained friends with Dempsey for the rest of his life, died June 27, 1990 in Reno. In his later years, Dempsey often flew to Sacramento to visit Ancil Hoffman and upon his arrival, he would nearly always place calls to Mrs. Abelman and Bill Graham, or drive to Reno to visit them. They both lived on California Avenue.

Deanna Piatelli Dempsey, the champion's fourth wife, died January 23, 2003 in New York City. After her husband's death in 1983, she established the Jack Dempsey Humanitarian Award, which is given out annually by St. Claire's Hospital in Manhattan. Jack Dempsey dedicated his 1977 autobiography to Deanna, saying simply: "To Deanna. Number Four should have been Number One … Thanks, honey."

Dick Evans, the former fighter and bar owner who wept as he watched films of Dempsey's fights after the champion's death, died in 1992. Still today, Evans' grandson, Jim Pace, keeps a photo of his grandfather with Jack Dempsey on the wall in his office at Reno High School.

Ty Cobb, the longtime Nevada newspaperman who probably wrote more words about Dempsey than any other Nevada writer, died May 25, 1997. During his 60-year career, he wrote dozens of columns and stories that included mention of Dempsey. That Cobb held tremendous respect for Dempsey was evident in a Dec. 31, 1967 column in which Cobb commented on a "computer fight" series that matched heavyweights of different eras. "It was an entertaining thing, but the final result, Rocky Marciano beating Jack Dempsey was hard for some of the ring purists to swallow. We disagree. It's a fact of nature that Marciano, 44, should have an edge over Dempsey, who's now 72."

Rollan Melton, one of the last, if not *the* last, Nevada writers to interview Dempsey, died January 10, 2001. After Dempsey's death, Melton recalled his first encounter with the Manassa Mauler and his emotions at the time. "Expecting to be dismissed quickly. Nervous. But with the champ, there was no need. He was as comfortable as worn shoes, as playful as a basket of puppies. That he was as famous as any American never turned his head or diluted his sensitivity to those who approached him." After Melton's death, many remembered him in those same terms.

Bill Pettite, a Reno native and associate of Max Baer's longtime manager Ancil Hoffman and the nephew of Nick and June Abelman, is retired and lives in Fair Oaks, Calif. He is one of the last living links between the boxers and managers of the early 20th Century and the present.

Bill Pettite Collection

Acknowledgements

Every journey begins with one step. In the case of this book, it started with one newspaper, a yellowed and fragile July 5, 1931 edition of the San Francisco Call-Bulletin. It was given to me by my friend Peter D. "Mick" Laxalt, who was born in 1931, but who held onto the paper for a different reason. It carried the story of a heavyweight boxing match between Paulino Uzcudun of Spain and Max Baer of Livermore, Calif., in Reno the previous day. Laxalt, the son of Basque immigrants, kept the paper for 75 years because his father, Dominique, had been in the crowd that day to witness his countryman, Uzcudun, win a 20-round decision under a blazing Nevada sun. While Baer and Uzcudun were the combatants that day, the true giant in the ring was Jack Dempsey, the Manassa Mauler himself, who was living in Reno at the time while awaiting a divorce.

Mick, whose brothers include former Nevada Governor and U.S. Senator Paul Laxalt and the late author Robert Laxalt, said he always wished someone would tell the story of Dempsey's time in Nevada. In past years, he had encouraged his brother, Robert, and the late Reno newspaperman Rollan Melton to take on the project, but time and other obligations kept them from it and they passed away before the story could be told. A couple of years ago, Mick asked me to consider it and gave me that old newspaper to get me started. It has been quite a journey from there and I'll be forever grateful to Mick for getting me started.

Mick's son Paul Laxalt, Joel Muller, Fred Davis, Roy Powers and Stan Warren have followed this project with great enthusiasm and support from the day it was born over lunch at the Gold 'n' Silver restaurant in Reno. We are all glad this story has been told at last.

I want to thank my friend and colleague Steve Sneddon, the longtime boxing writer for the *Reno Gazette-Journal*, who knows more about boxing and its history than anyone I know. That he was kind enough to write the foreword to this book means the world to me.

There are many others I need to thank for helping to make this book a reality, because without their efforts – and their love of history – it simply would have been impossible to achieve. My great thanks to Bill Pettite, who knew Dempsey, Ancil Hoffman, Max Baer and many other key figures personally; Bill Cobb and Ty Cobb Jr., who keep their father's history in Nevada a living one; Evelyn Pace and her son, Jim, who kept many of the historic artifacts from her father, Dick Evans, and the Eastside Inn, where Dempsey was a frequent visitor; Neal Cobb, who preserves photographs of old Reno; Bill Griswold, who keeps the artifacts of his later father, former Governor Morley Griswold; the grandchildren of former Governor Fred Balzar; Gary Schultz, a boxing memorabilia collector who loves to share; Marilyn Melton, my partner in two other Nevada books and a walking encyclopedia of Reno history; Nan Spina, Reno history buff; Pat McDonnell at the University of Nevada, Reno Communications Department; Dick Gammick, Washoe County's district attorney who met Dempsey as a youngster in Elko; and Colleen Rosencranzt, an angel to Dempsey's nephew Lloyd Stannard in his final years, who was generous enough to share her wonderful collection of photos and memorabilia. I would also like to thank F. A. Pettite and Marilyn Burson for their contributions.

A special thanks to Jack Dempsey's granddaughter, Erin O'Flaherty, for her help with family history.

Professional historians who aided this project include Loretta Filon at the Central Nevada Museum; Nevada State Archivist Guy Rocha; Eric Moody, Mella Harmon, Lee Brumbaugh and the staff at the Nevada Historical Society; Cheryl Carpenter at the Northeast Nevada Museum; Tom King, Mary Larson and the staff at the University of Nevada, Reno Oral History Program; and Dan and Dana Bennett of the Friends of Midas.

Several people helped me cut the red tape to get documents and photos critical to this story. Dianne Drinkwater, Kristin McQueary, Bryan Allison and I all worked together more than 20 years ago on the University of Nevada's college newspaper, Sagebrush. They are still good investigative reporters. Mike Mentaberry and his daughter, Molly, researched the home Jack Dempsey bought while living in Reno.

Sharon Genung and Jeannie Rasmussen are the caretakers of the *Reno Gazette-Journal* newsroom and library respectively and I could not have done this project without them.

I also owe thanks to Merrie Leininger, Stephanie Lauer, and Linsay Oakden, my vastly underpaid and much-appreciated copy editors; Christine Kelly, my advisor on all things book-related and friend on all things period; Natalie Chamberlain, my friend and No. 1 sounding board; and Jack Bacon, who agreed to publish this book based solely on faith.

My sister, Val, used her research abilities to find things I could not on my own. My parents, Miller and Lorraine Clifton, are the inspiration for everything I do.

My sincerest thanks to everyone who helped with this project.

Longtime Reno resident Buddy Garfinkle holds a photo of Jack Dempsey and himself taken in 1931 at the Reno Boxing Club. *Author's Collection*

About the Cover: Buddy's Story

In the summer of 1931, Buddy Garfinkle was a feisty 4-year-old and a fixture at the new Reno Boxing Club. His father, Imey, was a journeyman boxer who trained and fought at the club and who would later promote bouts there when it became known as the Chestnut Street Arena. "I used to sleep under the tables," Buddy recalled three quarters of a century later. "I got to know all the fighters."

One of those fighters was arguably the greatest heavyweight of them all – Jack Dempsey, the Manassa Mauler himself, who launched a comeback in August of 1931 in Reno, where he had made his home base. Dempsey trained at the gym and during one of those sessions, Imey Garfinkle put young Buddy in the ring with the champion. A photographer snapped the photo and an artist later hand-colored it. Buddy Garfinkle has kept it ever since.

Despite his early rearing in the pugilistic environment, Buddy did not follow his father or Jack Dempsey into a life in the ring. By the time he was 12, his parents had divorced and Buddy was on his own. He hawked newspapers, cleaned the slaughter room at the Nevada Packing Company and shined shoes in Douglas Alley. Among his shoeshine customers were Bill Graham and James McKay, who often talked business as the youngster worked away. Among his newspaper customers were the prostitutes who worked in "the cribs." They would often give him meals.

Buddy became a star athlete and student at Reno High School, playing quarterback in football and also excelling in basketball and baseball. He was also the school's student body president his senior year.

After graduating in 1944, he served in the Navy during World War II in the Pacific Theater. He returned to Reno after his discharge and went on to the University of Nevada. Again, he excelled in athletics and was a starter for legendary basketball coach Jake Lawlor.

From 1946 to 1952, as he was getting his bachelor's and masters degree, he was the recreation director for the city of Reno. In 1949, his first teaching job was at the grammar school he had attended himself, Orvis Ring. He then spent a year at Northside Junior High before joining the staff at Reno High School in 1951 where he coached the varsity basketball team and junior varsity football. His basketball teams won back-to-back state championships in the mid-1950s. He also coached two state champion American Legion baseball teams and served as a junior ski program instructor for several years.

He became a school administrator and was the principal at Echo Loder Elementary, Peavine Elementary, Clayton Middle School and Hug High School before retiring in 1970.

Along the way, he also served a term in the Nevada Assembly in the late 1960s.

Today, at age 80, Buddy Garfinkle remains a recreation enthusiast. He lives in Incline Village on the shores of Lake Tahoe where he plays tennis and paddles his kayak as much as possible. Like Jack Dempsey, who pedaled his bicycle in New York's Central Park at age 80, Garfinkle loves the feel of his body at work.

His philosophy these days is a simple one. "Live every day like it's your last and learn something new every day like you will live forever."

The Dempsey-Willard
Ring Bell

On the wall of a Reno restaurant, Jake's Place, owned by J.P. and Barbara Pinocchio, is a large wooden plaque with an ancient ring bell mounted on it. The bell is painted bright red, with a white horseshoe in the middle. Chipping paint reveals it was once painted yellow. On the top of the plaque are painted the words "July 4, 1919 Toledo, Ohio." Further down, and on both sides of the bell are the words, "Jack Dempsey-Jess Willard."

The bell once belonged to Reno saloon owner Dick Evans, a one-time middleweight boxer, who ran Dick & Ernie's Eastside Inn, along with his brother Ernie. Exactly how it came into his possession is lost to history, but Dempsey and Evans were longtime friends and whenever the Manassa Mauler was in Reno, he visited the Eastside Inn. Evans believed it was authentic. In a story about the bell that ran in the *Nevada Appeal* newspaper, he said he had been approached by the Boxing Hall of Fame to have it displayed there.

The question of the authenticity of the bell became the subject of an investigation of the PBS television show "The History Detectives" in 2006. Host Tukufu Zuberi and the show's research staff took on the task of proving or disproving whether this was the bell that failed to ring when Dempsey won the world title by pummeling Willard under a hot July sun in Toledo.

Interviews were conducted in Reno and New York City with boxing experts, including boxing historian Bert Sugar; Jack Kearns Jr., the son of Dempsey's longtime manager Doc Kearns; and with Dick Evans' daughter,

Ev Pace.   *Author's Collection*

What the investigators found? Maybe it is the bell and maybe it isn't.

As Zuberi revealed, the investigation also found a claim that the right bell from the fight was given to the Toledo fire chief in 1919 after Doc Kearns hired him to disrupt Jess Willard's night of sleep on the eve of the fight.

"When it comes to sports memorabilia, there is often more than one story," Zuberi said.

The question might never be answered. There are no known photos of the ring bell from the Dempsey-Willard fight and even if there were, they would likely prove inconclusive.

In the end, the Reno ring bell serves as a reminder of a great champion, a man of the West, and a friend to many in Nevada. It's one of the only tributes to Dempsey anywhere in the Silver State.

Dempsey's Nevada Fights

Date	Opponent	Site	Result
1915			
April 26	Anamas Campbell	Reno	KO3
May 31	Johnny Sudenberg	Goldfield	D10
July 11	Johnny Sudenberg	Tonopah	D10
1916			
Feb 5	Johnny Sudenberg	Ely	KO2
April 8	Joe Bond	Ely	W10
Oct. 7	Terry Keller	Ely	W10
1918			
Sept. 14	Jack Moran	Reno	KO1
1931			
Aug. 19	Jack Beasley	Reno	KO2
Sept. 7	Eddie Burns	Reno	Exh. 2
Sept. 7	Sam Baker	Reno	Exh. 2
Sept. 7	Red Tingley	Reno	KO2

Key: KO – Knockout; W – Win by decision; D – Draw; Exh. – Exhibition.

Sources: The Ring Record Book and Boxing Encyclopedia; *Reno Evening Gazette*; *Nevada State Journal*; *Tonopah Daily Bonanza*; *Goldfield Daily Tribune*; *White Pine News*; *Ely Record*.

Note: The Ring Record Book lists Dempsey's Tonopah fight with Johnny Sudenberg as a win for Dempsey. Newspaper accounts and Dempsey's 1950 autobiography both said it was a draw.

Bibliography

Books

Bennett, Dana R. *A Century of Enthusiasm: Midas, Nevada, 1907-2007*, Friends of Midas, Midas, Nev. 2007.

Cavanaugh, Jack. *Tunney: Boxing's Brainiest Champ and His Upset of the Great Jack Dempsey*. Random House, New York, 2006.

Cobb, Ty. *The Best of Cobbwebs*. The Black Rock Press, Reno, 1997.

Clifton, Guy. *Reno Rodeo: A History, The First 80 Years*. Reno Rodeo Foundation, Reno, 1999.

Dempsey, Jack, (With Bob Considine and Bill Slocum). *Dempsey: By The Man Himself*. Simon and Schuster, New York, 1959.

Dempsey Jack (With Barbara Piatelli Dempsey). *Dempsey*. Harper & Rowe, New York, 1977.

Dondero, Don (With Jean Stoess). *Dateline: RENO: Photography by D. Dondero*. Don Dondero, Reno, 1991.

Fleischer, Nat. *Nat Fleischer's The Ring Record Book and Boxing Encyclopedia*. The Ring Book Shop, New York, 1964.

Kahn, Roger. *A Flame of Pure Fire: Jack Dempsey and the Roaring '20s*. Harcourt Inc., Orlando, Fla., 1999.

Kling, Dwayne. *The Rise of the Biggest Little City: An Encyclopedic History of Reno Gaming, 1931-1981*. University of Nevada Press, Reno and Las Vegas, 2000.

Land, Barbara and Myrick. *A Short History of Reno*. University of Nevada Press, Reno and Las Vegas, 1996.

Melton, Rollan. *Nevadans*. University of Nevada Press, Reno and Las Vegas, 1988.

Moe, Albert Woods, *Nevada's Golden Age of Gambling*, Puget Sound Books, 2001.

Myles, Myrtle Tate. *Nevada's Governors: From Territorial Days to the Present 1861-1971*. Western Printing & Publishing Company, Sparks Nevada, 1972.

Smith, Toby. *Kid Blackie: Jack Dempsey's Colorado Days*. Wayfinder Press, Ouray, Colo., 1987.

Roberts, Randy. *Jack Dempsey: The Manassa Mauler*. University of Illinois Press, Chicago, 1979.

Newspapers and Wire Services

Reno Evening Gazette
Nevada State Journal
Reno Gazette-Journal
Fallon Standard
Battle Mountain Scout
The Humboldt Star
Goldfield Daily Tribune
Tonopah Daily Bonanza
The Ely Record
The Fallon Standard
White Pine News
Miami News
Elko Daily Free Press
Goldfield News and Beatty Bulletin
Tonopah Times-Bonanza
Nevada State Herald
New York Morning Telegraph
New York World
New York Tribune

New York American
New York Times
Ogden Daily Examiner
San Francisco Chronicle
Las Vegas Review-Journal
Las Vegas Sun
Los Angeles Times
The Associated Press
United Press International

Oral Histories

From the University of Nevada Oral History Program
John Cahlan
John Sanford
Lester B. "Benny" Binion
Thomas C. Wilson
Roger Teglia
Andrew Ginocchio
Edwin Cantlon
Rollan Melton
Midas, Nevada

Magazines

Old West
Sports Illustrated

Index

Chambers, Tom 18, 20
Chaplain, Charlie 37, 52, 47, 119
Charles, Ezzard 159
Charles, Pierre 160
Christian, George 19
Church, Elizabeth 71
Clark, Wilbur 134, 142, 162
Clarkson, Effie (sister) 40
Clift, Montgomery 145
Clinedinst, J. B. 107
Cobb, Ty (baseball) 85
Cobb, Ty (newspaper) 64, 87, 139, 154, 163
Cochran, Welker 85
Coffroth, Jim 56, 68
Cohen, George M. 46
Collins, Phil 119
Connolly, One-eyed 117
Cook, W. W. 121
Coolidge, Calvin 52
Copeland, George 136
Copeland, Jack 136
Corbett, Jim 108
Corbitt, Young III 140
Costello, Mike 121
Crafts, William 45
Craven, Thomas 149
Crawford, Joan 119
Cristner, K. O. 107
Cuddy, Jack 13
Cunningham, B. J. 90
Curtis, Roy 86

Dalitz, Moe 162
Dalrymple, K. D. 154
Daniels, Josephus 42
Davis, Sammy Jr. 145
Deer, John 130
DeLongchamps, Frederick 80, 86
Dempsey Jack (the Nonpareil) 2
Dempsey, Barbara (daughter) 129, 141, 154
Dempsey, Bernie (brother) 2, 17, 40, 74, 92, 95
Dempsey, Bruce (brother) 24
Dempsey, Celia (mother) 2, 41, 53, 70, 121
Dempsey, Deanna Piatelli (fourth wife) 142, 145, 148, 149, 155, 162
Dempsey, Effie (sister) 142
Dempsey, Elsie (sister) 74
Dempsey, Florence (sister) 8
Dempsey, Hyrum (father) 2, 32, 40

Dempsey, Joan (Daughter) 129, 141, 154
Dempsey, Joe (brother) 115
Dempsey, Johnny (brother) 2, 59
Dempsey, Maxine Cates (first wife) 21, 24, 35, 36, 37, 38, 39, 40, 41, 42, 159
Deschamps, Francois 44, 46
Di Bernadi, Rick 117
Diabolt Brothers 94
Dillard, J. C. 86
Dillard, Joe 89, 90
Dinsmore, Sanford C. 86
Dondero, Don 146, 147
Dooling, Maurice J. 40, 42
Dormio, Lena 102
Downey, Jack 17, 18
Doyle, Charles 146, 147, 149
Doyle, Howard S. 74
Drackert, Harry 114
Driscoll, Tommy 3, 4
Dunbar, Dorothy 88, 116
Durand, Marius 135, 136
Durham, John C. 106, 107, 115

Earp, Wyatt 25
Evans, Dick 139, 140, 151, 154, 163, 171
Evans, Ernie 139, 154, 171
Evans, Max 140
Everett, Buck 107

Fairbanks, Douglas 37, 52, 119
Fairbanks, Douglas Jr., 119
Farley, James 136
Farr, Johnny 70
Fields, Jackie 151
Fields, W.C. 85
Firpo, Luis Angel 49, 50, 51, 52, 56, 69, 107
Fitzsimmons, Bob 21, 25, 98, 108
Flinker, Sailor Jimmy 93
Flowers, John "Swede" 142, 143
Flynn, "Fireman Jimmy" 24
Flynn, Leo P. 59, 62, 64
Flynn, Leo 64
Ford, Henry 46
Ford, Tennessee Ernie 140
Foster, Ken 106
Frayne, Pat 86
Frisch, Roy 76
Fuente, Tony 90, 91
Fulton, Fred 24, 27, 41

This first edition of *Dempsey in Nevada*
is limited to a printing of 1500 copies.

Designed by Jim Richards.

The type is Janson.
The paper is Finch Opaque.

Dempsey in Nevada is a joint production of
Baobab Books and Jack Bacon & Company.